MEETUP TO MILLIONS

How to Grow a Meetup into a Global Community

James Mayes
Kiri Nowak-Smith

First edition
ISBN: 978-1-3999-9701-0

FOREWORD

Meetup to Millions is a book that matters today.

In a post-pandemic world where we are experiencing an epidemic of loneliness, the need to meet is felt by all generations.

Technology has helped us to get to know each other, but it has failed to connect us. Meeting new people for business or pleasure is incredibly challenging.

James' story and his Mind The Product journey show the power of in-person connections and how events are the most powerful tool for building community.

But the book goes further. It delivers a practical blueprint to elevate informal gatherings into structured events that generate value for all parties.

Whether you host running groups or AI meetups, this book will be your indispensable companion to grow your small group into a structured community.

It will also transform your informal meetup into an event. I can't wait to welcome you to the event industry, a $1.3 trillion industry whose objective is to connect people.

James delivered an essential piece on how modern events form.

Dig in and start building!

— Julius Solaris
Founder, Boldpush

PREFACE

This is a story I've been wanting to write for many years. I originally envisaged it as the story of Mind the Product, but in these post COVID years there's a deep need to rebuild communities, so we've gone far deeper into those elements.

For reasons I'll explain, this first edition is a guide to both getting started and some best practices in community building. We'll ask you to consider the journey from small events to global empire, and we'll start by helping you lay strong foundations. On my journey, Mind the Product became a global media and events business, but the roots and still the strength of that firm lay in the community foundations we laid first. We had no idea it would become so successful but since it did, I'm delighted to share those learnings here.

This book is also intended to inspire, to show just how far this journey might take you. This is a tale from someone who has already scaled this kind of business globally, so contains many key lessons on things I would do differently now. With this book you get the gift of a decade of expensive hindsight!

Since Kiri and I started this project, something else has come to light. In January 2024 I was diagnosed with a brain tumour, so I've been through surgery and am currently in secondary treatment for that. That has certainly impacted available time and energy levels a little. With this fresh challenge in mind, we will be back with a second edition -

but first, we wanted to get what we have now out into reader's hands, and I'm keen to hear your feedback.

In the next edition we will then take a deeper dive and show you how you're going to scale for global domination, reaping the bigger rewards of an international media and events empire, if that's your goal!

Do find me on LinkedIn[1] if you have any questions or feedback, I'm always keen to listen.

— James Mayes

THE ORIGIN STORY: FROM A SMALL PUB MEETUP TO WORLDWIDE EVENTS...

Picture this: 25 product managers walk into a bar.

Their aim? To casually chat about the challenges of product management.

Sipping on drinks whilst exchanging product stories and the difficulties of getting things signed off with management. The setting may have been humble but their enthusiasm for all things product went through the roof.

Not exactly groundbreaking, is it?

But this chance meeting was meant to be. It was the catalyst for something much bigger and more powerful.

It snowballed into a worldwide event series and 300,000 strong community of product managers. Who knew that a tiny casual meetup had so much potential? Often in life, it's the little things that snowball into something unimaginable.

In this book, I'll tell you exactly how Mind The Product (MTP)[3] came to be. Plus, we'll offer invaluable tips and advice on how to achieve something similar and tell you about an exciting project that's in the pipeline... (the best excuse to read on - trust us). We'll also explore some successful community case studies and share some invaluable advice from their founders. These people have been there and done it – and they've got a wealth of knowledge to share. Knowledge that will help you to grow your own community.

With MTP, the concept was so simple. Surely a friendly gathering in a pub couldn't become much more than a casual brainstorm? Little did we know back then how spot on we were with the timing. There was definitely a growing need for PM's (Product Managers) to come together.

But the reality was that in the early 2000's, product managers perhaps weren't as prominent within organisations as they should have been. It has taken a while.

It's fair to say that product management first appeared on the scene in 1931. Neil H. McElroy of Procter & Gamble created a shift in thinking towards brand management and product managers. Though way back then, he described product managers as 'brand men.'[4]

Hewlett-Packard were another early pioneer for product managers, introducing a division structure with different product groups who developed, manufactured and marketed products.

But despite a clear role emerging, product managers were just part of the marketing or engineering teams. It's only really very recently that separate departments have been created solely for product management. Back when MTP started, we didn't yet have a seat at the big table. But we knew this needed to change.

Over time, more businesses have realised that somebody in their organisation needs to steer products in the right direction.

Interest in the role grew and as such, so did the need for a platform for product managers to communicate, share tips and keep track of the latest news.

Initially, technology product managers appeared almost exclusively in startup firms – but these firms demonstrated how product people enabled them to move faster. More and more established companies like banks and telecoms firms were starting to bring more formal product roles too. Mind the Product undoubtedly benefited from this market shift.

The secret to success? Throw out the assumption of some complex formula.

If you ask us, it's ***community***.

The art of togetherness, the shoulder to lean on, the thumbs up to your next big idea. Hear me out...

Have you ever had those days where you're gazing through the window, longing for a group of passionate people to pick at and creative minds to inspire you?

Well, back in 2010, Martin Erikkson had one of those moments, and with a little inspiration from Huddle's DrinkTank (an amazing networking group), he created the first-ever London ProductTank meet-up[5] – aimed at all things product. It took place in a back room of the Ruby Blue pub[6].

Product managers were united by one mission – to help drive forward their work and ultimately create products people love. The MTP Tagline is: *"Build Products Customer Love"*.

Minds united, ideas bloomed, and a hell of a lot of passion was shared – the professional kind, at least!

It was here that the fire was truly lit when Martin first had the pleasure of connecting with Janna Bastow[7] and Simon Cast[8].

Like Martin, they, too, had been yearning for a product-focused community meet-up.

Simon & Janna met around 2009 at a "Tweetup". In case you're wondering, "Tweetups" were occasional random gatherings of early Twitter (now X) users with aligned interests.

They started discussing the idea of a ProductCamp Day, or Product Management Unconference on the Barcamp[9].

It was around that time that someone connected them with Marin Eriksson, who was looking at arranging an evening meetup for Product Managers. The three agreed to work together.

Matt Hobbs[10] was one of the attendees at that first ever meet. At the time, he was a brand-new face in the product management scene, and now he's blossomed to become the Chief Product Officer for a breakthrough financial services company.

He described that inaugural session as *"engaging and good fun - plus free beer - so I was hooked and in for almost every event after that."* And we have to agree with him, who doesn't love a free drink amongst like-minded folk?

Selena Hadzibabic[11] was another of the friendly faces who showed up that evening, and drawing on the night's memories, she said it felt *"like finding an oasis"*.

Now a product leader over in NYC, she recalled, *"Janna and I had met earlier and wondered where the heck all the product managers in this town were and why there wasn't any kind of community"*.

And right there, in that very sentence, is what kick-started Mind The Product's mission and continues to drive it into the success it is today.

After that fateful day in the pub, their desire only grew stronger as they realised just how beneficial something like this could be.

Well, it wasn't long before the trio aligned their energy to make their dreams an incredible reality.

The first step in their collaboration together? The first-of-its-kind platform made for product people by product people.

And, so it was born – Mind the Product – a blog adorned with rich, powerful content and driven by a desire to inspire, educate and inform. And, if you ask me, that's just what it did.

The name was dreamt up over the clinking of drinks one evening when the trio met in Kingly Court, London. It gives a nod to the company's roots in the capital of England, and like any London commuter will know – the please mind the gap message that rings through our ears at each station.

It's 2012, and the blog was (and still is) pulling in product people from near and far, but now was the time to take a leap of faith: The very first Mind the Product conference.

The Birth of the Conference

The ProductTank meetups began in 2010 in London and operated pretty reliably every month as a community free to attend event. For those first couple years, building the community audience happened beautifully organically. Our audience was asking for more, and the early team had ambitions to meet that. Then one of the attendees said: *"Wouldn't it be great to hear some speakers in London share their experience in the Valley!"*

Well, that involves paying for their flights and hotels, so we'd need to fund that somehow. If we charge for tickets, that would work.... and so a conference was born! It was launched in 2011 and happened in 2012.

The community group already had several thousand members with several hundred turning up every time for the meetups; they were often over-subscribed! At that point, the team was confident that tickets would sell. We had great speaker connections, we'd tested a number of them at those community events, so our confidence was solid.

The next key decision was around the venue. The team purposely chose something tight enough that it wasn't going to be too much of a stretch, with a capacity cap of 450 people. We were regularly getting 300-400 people trying to attend the Meetup, and a full-blown conference would have a much more compelling lineup of speakers.

The hairy factor actually came with the after-party that we planned. In which you learn the lesson that when something goes wrong in events, it does so expensively. It's very rarely just a couple of hundred pounds. It's more likely a couple of thousand. In our case, an after-party venue had been chosen, and a ten thousand pound deposit had been paid a few months in advance.

The bar went bust just before the event, and we never saw the money again. So, that was uncomfortable and a hard lesson to learn. And probably the single biggest hiccup with that first conference. There was a hard scramble and an alternative was found, but the buffer we thought existed on ticket and sponsor revenue took a real hit!

It was held at the Mermaid Conference Centre in London. The team waited on tenterhooks as, one by one, over 450 people piled through the doors – each eager to meet others on the same wavelength, take inspiration for a better BAU and be a part of something special: To be inspired by speakers from heart Silicon Valley, a community, our community.

The conference was a triumph, and in no time, #mtpcon became the next big thing – and, as some have said, *"a therapy session for logic-starved product folks"*.

It was at this time I (James Mayes!) joined the journey, stepping up to become the fourth co-founder. I brought a wealth of knowledge on all things commercial to the table.

At the same time ProductTank continued to grow, creeping out of the confines of the M25, the border to the city that had already magnified our hopes into something much more – and popping up in Manchester and over in Amsterdam too.

More and more product people were finding each other, and they, too, appreciated the strength of togetherness – asking to run their own ProductTank sessions.

ProductTank had grown into something more than the team could have ever imagined – it was now global. Enter Marc Abraham[12]. Or, should we say hail, Marc Abraham.

The next member of our dream team, reigning in control of ProductTank's international coordination and keeping the team calmly organised (something the team definitely needed through the craziness of its growth!).

Time check – it's now 2014, and Mind The Product's loyal followers are eager to keep learning and keen to become the most knowledgeable product experts.

And so, the team added workshops to the #mtpcon repertoire; these hands-on learning experiences allowed each and every member to get fully immersed. But also to smooth cash flow and responses to customers' needs.

By the time the year had passed, the range of London conferences (including ones held in the Barbican - all Londoners will get why this is a proud moment for me!) had continued to expand. MTP had grown an army of over 1000 attendees tagging along to hear great talks. and learn from others' experiences.

ProductTank had also firmly secured its home in cities all over the globe. So naturally, the next place to cement its place was the States, starting in sunny San Francisco, on the doorstep of the holy grail of product innovation - Silicon Valley.

'GIGAOM Roadmap Conference'[13] is one of the other product giants that had tried and failed before. The team apprehensively entered the US scene, but it turns out there was no need for nerves. Instead, I, for one, was instantly blown away. And apparently, so was our stateside community.

The Creation of Our Workshops and San Francisco Expansion

When we first Incorporated, the company behind ProductTank was actually named the European Product Managers Group, which would suggest ambitions certainly weren't global back then! In 2013, we renamed that to Mind the Product Limited, to align with the conference, represent the greater ambitions and give a stronger, clearer brand name.

We also started considering workshops. We wanted to diversify the revenue stream a little bit and see what else we could offer the community that they might value. And we learnt that a number of people who were constantly attending the events were doing so for professional learning and that they had professional budgets available for this. We could solve their problem and ours!

So, at the 2014 conference, we introduced the first workshops. We didn't have our own training materials at this point, but we knew a number of great people in the market who delivered training to companies. So we approached a small group of them: *"If we can provide classroom environments alongside the conferences, and we can sell tickets, would you be interested in delivering a session for a fair payment?"*

We persuaded a bunch of people to come on board with us and do exactly that. Our team sold the tickets and arranged the classrooms. Guest presenters came along and delivered those workshops, and we happily split the proceeds.

In 2015, after lengthy deliberations, we took the conference to the US for the first time. This was something that made the team very, very uncomfortable. It was a big risk. We recognise that we were essentially a London-based crew going to San Francisco, the heart of technology, and telling them how to do this, right? Was it a pipe dream? Well, we wouldn't find out unless we tried.

I'll be honest; we were just a little bit worried. We thought long and hard about how we could test this without creating too much risk. We'd asked folks in the US if they could run ProductTank meetups there, so a little community building had already started. What's more, we could see US traffic heating the website to catch the best of the content from the London event! Our first challenge? To find a low-risk way of seeing if the market is interested!

So we had a conversation as a team and decided we were prepared to put a couple of thousand dollars down as a venue deposit and talk to a few friends who had spoken for us at the event in London.

Once you have the venue name and a date and a few of those early speaker names confirmed, you can then launch a site. You can say to people, this conference will be happening on this date. That's enough to get some early bird tickets on sale and start talking to sponsors to test their interest too.

We agreed that if we could sell a few hundred tickets within the first month or two, that would give us enough confidence to really commit and run the thing. So we put a couple hundred early bird tickets on sale for that first conference and were blown away by the result.

It actually got to the point where a couple of people on the team were calling each other to ask if there was something wrong – there were no tickets left to sell! Did we break something? Did we do something wrong? No, it wasn't down or broke: we'd sold out! We sold those early bird tickets in literally four seconds. Plus, we had 700 additional eager product people added to the long waiting list. We looked on in disbelief!

It turned out that the work we'd done in both London and San Francisco to build community, to capture the content from those London events and put that online that gave people confidence. Enough confidence that they had no hesitation in buying the tickets. This was an absolute game changer..

That first conference in 2015 in San Francisco[14] was the thing that gave us the confidence to take the whole business much more seriously. It was at the end of 2015 that Martin and I actually went full-time! This had always been the thing that we'd done, evenings and weekends. Perhaps an occasional day off work here and there. It had all been side hustle style. It hadn't been a main job for us. 2015 was the turning point. That U.S. conference changed everything.

Germany

Following this instant success in San Francisco, we wanted to bring the same excitement to Germany by hosting a regional conference, and in 2017, we did just that. Born of ProductTank Hamburg[15] organisers.

MTP Engage[16] took place in Hamburg, and it marked the first major gathering (and the biggest turnout) of product people that Germany had ever seen.

At the same time, requests were rolling in for Mind The Product to provide corporate training, hoping that it could bring one-of-a-kind workshops to life in-house. And so, that's what the team did. The first of our dedicated team training programmes was in partnership with C. Todd Lombardo[17] for Telenor in Oslo.

Marking eight wonderful years since the humble beginnings of that very first meet-up at an unassuming London pub, the team decided to launch and celebrate World Product Day on May 23rd. It saw the extended Mind the Product family run over 90 in-person events held in locations all over the globe.

After the success in SF in 2015, we were ready to start looking at other options to expand. In Europe, Germany looked to be the most exciting market, and we knew a few hundred community members from the German meetups came to the annual London conference.

We already had meetups established in multiple cities in Germany (Berlin, Dusseldorf, Frankfurt, Hamburg and more) so at one of the London conferences I invited the organisers of meetups in Germany to come talk more with me about the potential for a conference there.

It quickly became apparent that Hamburg would be our target of choice. With a fast growing startup scene, Berlin was already really busy with other tech conferences. We felt like the Hamburg organisers really understood what we wanted to achieve, there was plenty of shared vision going on.

We revised the brand to "MTP Engage" - to lean on the Mind the Product brand, but also to differentiate from the full flagship conference and to lean into more local engagement.

Our team in London would provide significant support in both designing and marketing this new event, but our community leads in Hamburg would lead on things like local knowledge (finding the venue) and the speaker curation.

After all, they knew the regional community best, and we wanted to reflect that in the agenda. Over the years, a wonderful event developed as MTP Engage Hamburg. It was so successful that gradually other local organisers asked if they could replicate it! A few years later, we did exactly that, this time with MTP Engage Manchester. Same model, partnering with the local organisers and supporting centrally.

Meanwhile, the launch of ProductTanks spanning across the Asia-Pacific region saw the opportunity to launch #mtpcon here too. Not long after, we launched our opening conference at the iconic Victoria Theatre in Singapore in 2016.

So, to recap. Where are we now, in 2024? From our humble meet in a pub off of Ruby Blue in London, we've grown into the world's largest community of product people, with over 300,000 members (and we're still growing too).

The onboarding of fresh new faces brings exciting new talent, groundbreaking new ideas and inspiration in the form of tonnes of world-class content, invaluable product training and engaging conferences.

Now that's what we call community. That's what we call a success story. Intrigued? I'm honoured to be able to show you the ropes and how you can do the same.

JAMES MAYES: MY STORY

Hi, I'm James Mayes. We may have met before; you might have been by my side for parts of my story, or we may be total strangers. That's OK, though, because here's the part where you get to know a bit more about me and what makes me tick. Here's the story of James Mayes: the story of me.

As you might know, I was the fourth person to join the Mind The Product team as a co-founder. The first three were Simon, Janna and Martin.

My foray into the business world began over 27 years ago now, so I'm definitely not a newbie, but I wouldn't class myself as an old boy... yet. With that, you can probably envisage I've had my fair share of experiencing the ups and downs of everything this busy, ever-changing environment has to offer.

I'm incredibly proud to have been a part of some groundbreaking projects, but that doesn't mean these feats come effortlessly. It's fair to say some were certainly harder than others.

In fact, with every success comes painstaking lows, personal battles and a million challenges along the road.

However, everything that has stood in my way has in itself twisted and turned and led me down the path to where I stand today. The sweet spot. So I guess I can't complain, really (thank you, universe)!

And who wants to read a plain sailing story with no windy seas? It's the challenges that make life *interesting*. I love this quote by lyricist and novelist Paulo Coelho. It's particularly applicable to business...

> *"Not all storms come to disrupt your life; some come to clear your path."*
>
> —Paulo Coelho

I guess you might be wondering how I got to this point. Before I get into the nitty-gritty of how to build a community, let's touch on my personal story. It links into everything I've achieved professionally, so I thought it was worth a mention. Often it's the personal story that everyone is interested in anyway!

So, let's dive in, shall we? Juicy details and all...

Little James

To really get to know me, though, we have to rewind the clock – all the way back to when I was a boy – little James, if you will.

I had a wonderful childhood growing up in the beautiful English countryside, just a stone's throw away from the Stonehenge monument. You can just picture it, right? Idyllic.

Looking back now, it was completely dreamy, but everyone knows that kids have their heads absorbed in other things (ahem, meeting friends at the park, trading their adored football card collection, playing conkers – need I go on?). I perhaps didn't appreciate it at the time as much as I do now.

I filled my days riding horses (I worked at the local farmyard) and chasing my little brother around the vast green landscape that circled my family home. I didn't live in a castle, far from it. We had a modest bungalow in a small village called Amesbury.

The years rolled by, and by the time I hit the awkward teenage years, my family and I moved from the countryside to Portsmouth for my father's job.

No kid (or adult, for that matter!) enjoys being uprooted: Uprooted from friends, memories, and places that you hold close to your heart. But I took the move in my stride. I switched out bartering farmers for horses to ride and then bartering with boat owners who needed crew. The open fields, country air and hay bales simply turned to sea, sand and salty hair.

My parents worked tirelessly to provide us with an enriched life one that I, of course, am eternally grateful for. It meant they were often working multiple jobs and busy earning extra pounds to make sure me and my brother never went without.

At the time, my father worked in manufacturing. It wasn't the best time to be in this realm – the UK manufacturing industry was imploding, so he got made redundant on multiple occasions. My mum worked an array of things, including running her own fitness business, then taking on a busy seafront guest house, and finally moving into financial services!

As a family unit, it was tough going. It meant we'd often have to move to new towns to chase employment. Each time I'd start off once again as the newbie in school and had to rebuild new friendships (which isn't always easy as the new kid on the block!).

It, however, did mean that I became a self-claimed pro at adapting to new environments and ever-changing landscapes – it's one of my strengths even today. Proof that our successes can be born from the most challenging situations.

I've always battled imposter syndrome which meant I used to be quite shy. It came from moving around a lot when I was younger, always being the new kid at school. As I became more established and knowledgeable on the event scene, I overcame that. It was a learned skill though, a muscle that needs to be trained and exercised regularly.

Another skill that saw me sail through school without too much fuss was my ability to be able to join the dots quickly. I quickly saw how different subjects could relate to one another. By pulling appropriate examples from one stream of study into another, I was able to explore areas teachers considered less obvious and that meant they took deep interest in whatever I wanted to contribute, which in turn built my confidence.

This is a trait I'm so happy has stayed with me throughout the years, and probably has its roots in my own neuro diversity! Although it can sometimes be a huge distraction, finding these opportunities has also created unexpected and valuable outcomes on so many occasions.

Someone once told me that I join dots in a way others don't see. I still think of this as a superpower!

Hand in hand with my adaptability and dot-joining came my natural tendency to be a bit of a chatterbox. I found it pretty easy to make new connections and link my way into different friendship circles.

This skill bagged me my first Saturday job at a boating supplies shop. A huge plus for me because, as well as earning a few extra pounds at the weekend, it meant I had access to the boats too (every teenager's dream - sailing boats I'd only dream of).

Moving here, there, and everywhere so often when I was younger set me up to be brave, and independent and to put myself out there. I'd forever be meeting new people – and although I didn't realise it at the time, it definitely set me up for my future life in events management. Who knows? Maybe it is all written out in the stars.

A Step into the Professional World

Years passed, and I graduated from Middlesex University with a bit of an all-sorts degree. It had elements of geography, UK economics, environment, society, management information systems and more. So, with a wealth of knowledge under my belt, I wrote to a few recruitment agencies, and, as if by magic (or, more likely, hard work and determination), one hired me!

Professional life was going superbly – I was finally mixing in the business world, meeting new faces and developing on all of the skills I'd learnt from when I was just a boy.

My career in recruitment is worthy of a special note too. As anyone who's excelled (or stumbled through) the recruitment scene will know it's a tough and thankless job. And if you haven't, you can take it from me! It's no secret –

many people don't last, but those who do will face day-to-day struggles and come out of it with a wealth of benefits.

I, for one, did – it encourages you to connect with people from all walks of life, to evolve your understanding of every commercial level and problem-solve like no other role really does. It gives you a taste for marketing and sales, teaches you to negotiate, and can be a harsh taskmaster, too, full of rejections. For a first career, I regret nothing – because honestly? There's nothing like being thrown in at the deep end (as long as you can paddle a little!).

Some people in life will inadvertently leave a lasting imprint on your memory. And for me one of those people was one of my earlier recruitment managers. He was an ex-Army guy and introduced me to the idea of management by exception. He taught me clear operating parameters, huge amounts of freedom within that and absolutely zero micro-management. Long term, it wasn't perfect for me, but after being micromanaged for years previously, it was such a breath of fresh air. The kind of fresh air that is much welcomed in the business scene.

In 1996, I even went on to build the first team of Java developers in Europe, for IBM's research labs at Hursley Park. Although I wasn't a technical person at this point, I learnt enough jargon and specialist details along the way to have conversations. I remained in the industry for another 15 years before the start-up bug bit me... drum roll...

Get Set, Start-Up

Here it is – the turning curve in my professional life. The stab in the dark. The craving for a successful start-up.

Enter – TweetJobs. This was my very first start-up, and to cut to the chase, it was a quick failure.

But let's backtrack a little. I'd been in recruiting for quite some time, and with a passion in my soul for start-ups sitting on the back burner, it wouldn't take much for me to delve straight in. I, for one, love a new challenge.

That's when a former colleague, Richard Sutcliffe, approached me with the idea of a recruitment service based around social media giant Twitter (back in the good old years of Twitter, promise!).

Together, Richard and I raised some angel investment funds between us and set out on bringing our product to life. It was our first foray into startups – and simply put, we weren't first-time lucky. In fact, quite the opposite. We made all the mistakes (or many) along the way – even now, while I'm deep in reflection and reminiscing on past endeavours, I find more and more learning curves to take from it.

We didn't spend enough time really understanding what our customers actually wanted. We were too distant from them, but with MTP we could be up close and personal with our potential customers constantly, so we pushed ourselves to constantly ask them what else we might do that they'd value. If anything, this gave us a very different problem - we constantly had a huge list of things we wanted to go do next, and were often guilty of trying to do too much.

So, where did it all go wrong?

First of all, we didn't do enough customer discovery. We were also way too early to market, and in our rush to raise funds, we found we hadn't even scratched the surface in discovering the different types of investors and what they could each bring to the table.

Hindsight is a beautiful thing, isn't it? And looking back, the whole experience was genuinely eye-opening. My very first start-up adventure may have crashed and burned, but it gave me the flame of desire to keep pursuing that dream: to keep exploring new opportunities.

And that's what I did.

I hopped straight on over to another start-up, Brave New Talent.

They were a tech start-up in the recruiting space, one that had already got a few years into their journey. As such, I wrongly presumed they had a few more things figured out, and it would be a good place to settle straight in while learning what an early-stage start-up looked like.

In reality, what followed was another series of mishaps. There's a founder out there, who, like me, may want to tell his own story one day, but until then, I'll just say I learnt an awful lot here, too and had the opportunity to meet so many like-minded, knowledgeable people.

At least two other startups came from others that worked at Brave New Talent. You couldn't fault the phenomenal energy of the team and, indeed, the London startup scene in general at that time. It's been responsible for so many good things that have come since, and in a phrase I've heard from countless product people since, *"experiments are only a failure if you fail to learn"*.

The Cold Hard Truth

Most businesses fail. Investors know this better than most, and they play the numbers. They place their bets accordingly, in the knowledge that 90% of startups fail, 10% [18] within the first year!

> *"A broad set of stakeholders, including employees, strategic partners, and investors, all can play a role in a venture's downfall."*

> —Tom Eisenmann, Harvard Business Review, 2021. (Why Start-Ups Fail)[19]

At both TweetJobs and Brave New Talent, there was so much talent – so many good technical brains combined. But ultimately, they weren't delivering the customer with what they wanted, and that's what led to their failures.

One thing I can thank these failures for, though, is for giving me such a deep interest in good product management. It struck me as a crucial discipline and one of the most interesting roles that the tech world has to offer. I suppose it led (in part!) to me spending the rest of the next decade with Mind The Product.

It's a tale as old as time – before people have huge success, they often have rather epic failures. You may know the saying, *"Fall down seven times, stand up eight"*.

For obvious reasons (shame, embarrassment), people don't want to talk about business failures. It's what makes our stories, though and lucky you - you get to hear mine! But, in seriousness, our failures are a hugely important part of learning the ropes and getting a proper taste of the real world. Plus, no one loves a braggard – share the downs as well as the ups.

The Light at the End of the Tunnel

I'll admit that when I started out, I had a stab at two different businesses, and frustratingly, they both tanked. Yup. That was painful. I've learnt that I'm certainly an optimist - an optimist who always carries a raincoat, though.

But to quote Gerry and The Pacemakers (Liverpool fans rejoice), *"at the end of the storm, there's a golden sky"*, and my storm (the failure of that second business) actually put me in touch with ProductTank, the meetup for Product Managers and where it all began.

One of the biggest reasons that earlier business failed was because as founders, we simply didn't understand our customers' needs well enough. After learning that Product Managers were actually at the heart of those for many startups, I was motivated to spend more time hanging around them, learning from them.

The team behind ProductTank (Janna, Simon and Martin) were looking to level it up into the first Mind the Product conference, which was to be held at the Mermaid Centre in London in 2012. Three minds collided – Janna, Simon and Martin.

I put in my two cents and offered some commercial thoughts. Over time, they trusted what I said, I delivered, and I was able to add more to the mix. Of course, I was absolutely delighted to.

Not only was this audience in huge demand by recruiters, it was also a key decision making audience in the tech startup world. This made it a group software vendors really want to reach, and that desire could help create commercial sustainability. Over time, we investigated still further:

reasoning that these people gave up their time to come and learn from us. Perhaps they would be willing to spend money on more formal training. We explored numerous models and gradually built a very successful and scalable business.

I loved events, and I loved the vibe of building a community. It was infectious. I felt the Product Manager role was a niche of fast-growing importance, and it felt like a really interesting moment to be involved. And, so, it turned out that way. Then, in 2015 I was appointed as CEO, a role I held through to the sale to Pendo in 2022[20].

With all the passion, light and success that Mind The Product brought to my life, one undoubtedly huge benefit of it all was to work alongside the outstanding crew. I've been very lucky to meet so many people along the journey (too many to name personally!), and to hear some stellar speakers on stages across the world from London, San Francisco, Singapore and beyond.

Where Do I Go from Here?

Mind the Product achieved great things, and even now, since stepping back from this part of my journey, I still get many messages from people in that space thanking me for the impact it had on their professional lives, their career trajectories and overall success. Win-win all around!

I believe Mind The Product's success, though, wasn't achieved because of its tech stack but actually in spite of it.

Tech fought us throughout every step of the journey. In modern life, we have so many hacks and workarounds in day-to-day business, so many data manipulations and manual processes. I believe that making all of this quality content more widely available, validating its origins and connecting peers through the community for professional support (professional therapy?!) tied together the loop. So many tech platforms in this space never get past first-order thinking, so I'll be exploring that for the next few years! Psst... Bookmark https://howdy.rodeo/organizer/[21] for now (and thank me later) - it's not only the launch page for the book you're now reading, it's where we're gathering the names of those who'd like to hear how we'll solve some of these problems.

For this next phase in my journey, the lessons learned, and the friends that I've had the pleasure of meeting along the way are undoubtedly my secret weapon to future success!

There are so many amazing individuals who have helped, supported and been there for me along the way – I'd love to name them all personally, but it might take up a whole chapter, so for now, you know who you are and thank you. I completely recognise how lucky I am to have spent time with such great people.

So, if you want to take something from my life story to help you a little along your own journey - take my own accounts of my fearless endeavours along with this piece of advice that I've borrowed from William Durant, as he rather eloquently put it:

> *"Forget past mistakes. Forget Failures. Forget everything except what you're going to do now, and do it."*

—William Durant

BUILD YOUR OWN COMMUNITY: A NINE STEP ACTION PLAN BLUEPRINT

You've read about how MTP was started. I've filled you in on (the ups and downs of) our journey. And you've heard about my personal story. So now – it's about putting all of it together. It's time for an action plan. Something you can use right now to get your community started and continue to grow it.

I'm serving this up earlier in the book so you've got fast access to something actionable. You can literally take this blueprint and use it to launch into action – right now. We'll explore some of the finer details of growing, building, maintaining and eventually selling your community later on in the book.

We didn't have anything like this when we went on our MTP journey. We learned as we went along. But what if you're able to start out with a 'build your own community' action plan in your hands? Now wouldn't that be helpful?

I've wracked my brain, looked back at everything we did and pinpointed the key things that are needed to build a successful community. I wanted to create something actionable that can help people lay the foundations and journey fourth feeling empowered. You really can build your own community by following these nine core steps.

Of course, this is an idealistic view, and you may come across some 'road closures' and obstacles along the way (we'll touch on how to overcome those later). But that's OK – nuances are fine. As long as you stick to the main structure of the action plan, you'll have a robust and loyal group of followers in no time. So now, it's over to you. Communities reflect individuals, nuance and differences are to be expected.

Below is my extensive step-by-step blueprint for achieving a strong community.

1. The First Meetup

All hail the inaugural meetup. This is your chance for the all-important first impression. Want to learn how to pull off a brilliant first event? Flick forward to chapter 5 and take some notes on how to craft your first event (and make it one to remember!).

Ready to build your community? You'll need to begin with the legendary first meetup. It's time to gather a group of like-minded people who share the same passions and create an event to remember. This is an exciting time when you start to plan your first meetup.

You're probably wondering how it will go, what it will be like and where you'll go from there. Well, my advice is don't overthink it for too long, or you'll never get off the ground. The first event will help shape the future of your community. Follow my tips from Chapter 5, and your first event will be a hit.

2. Launch Additional Meetups

You've set an impeccable standard – now follow through with more intriguing, eye-opening, peer-supporting meetups. This is the best way to keep the momentum going. One, you'll always be in the front and centre of each individual's mind, and two, there will always be something exciting for your community to discover next.

So now it's time to start planning more meetups and creating some consistency with the events you deliver, whether that's online, offline or both! To grow your community, you need to have a future event for people to look forward to and focus on. Whether you choose to do two a month or two a year is up to you. Just make sure you've got something in the diary and a future vision for your community brand.

3. Content Site Creation

Be seen and be known. The best way of doing this? Aligning all of your content and plans into one place: your very own website.

There are a plethora of benefits to doing this. First of all, it gives you a handy place to direct interested members/sponsors about upcoming events and community news. You can also use your site to promote the group – it's simple to ping people over your web address.

Remember what I said about sending newsletters and utilising social media? By having a site – you can pack the copy with internal links for more information and have a place to keep all of it organised.

Have a decent amount of visits? Perfect. You could even look at monetising from your site and displaying sponsored content and advertising. But this shouldn't be what your site is about. It should be about providing value to your audience, not selling stuff. You want to create a helpful space for people to utilise and learn from.

When you talk about building a community, people always picture large-scale events. But growing a dedicated community online is a huge asset. You can also use your website to promote and discuss upcoming events and keep the conversation going after each event finishes.

Things to keep in mind? Ensure everything is user-friendly, and choose a design that is easy to navigate. If you want to attract new members, consider doing basic keyword research and find out what topics your audience is searching for. Keep an eye on Rodeo here, by making sure you're on this mailing list[22]. We never did find tooling we were completely happy with, and that's what I'm building now!

4. Get Set for Conferences

After a small while, you'll have a strong, regular meetup going ahead. Your events may have grown from a few loyal followers to a hundred or so eager attendees. Maybe you've outgrown your regular venue. Maybe you've got a bigger demand from different regions. When this is the case – it's time to launch your first conference.

Building a conference from the ground up is much the same as building a meetup. You need to outreach, promote and plan every aspect. Just at a grander scale, of course.

By this point, you'll most likely be part of a team, not a sole ranger. This makes the planning more manageable, as everyone will have their set roles. Someone to plan the logistics, another person to market tickets and maybe event sponsors, and another for the speakers and content plan ideally. These roles could be further split out, and will if you grow, but these are the core considerations.

5. Develop Growth Strategy

You and your team can now focus on how you grow going forward.

Take a look at the current market – where are their gaps? And how can you fill them?

A basic event strategy would involve planning, launching and promoting your events. But we're not just hosting events here, remember? The plan is to curate a community.

An army of loyal followers who want to spread the community vibe far and wide.

You'll need to develop some tools for growing your audience, which includes things like training workshops, online blog content, email newsletters, community chat platforms (WhatsApp, Facebook, LinkedIn, etc.) and event promotion.

Now is a good time to either invest in some marketing or put time into it yourself. The main thing you need to remember is that communities tend to grow from word of mouth, and you need a few people who will champion your brand.

6. Curate Training Content

So you've done your small-scale meetups, and you've dipped your toes in the large event pool. Maybe you've hosted a few conferences, and you're making a name for yourself. What can you do now to become more of an authority? Training content. It's invaluable to your community. It's another reason for them to come together and learn.

It's like a meetup but far more structured, and people come to learn about something specific. So have a think, what topics are you an authority on? Do you know some excellent training delivery people who can take your training sessions to the next level? And don't forget, once you've held a training session, make sure you repurpose the content elsewhere.

What do I mean by this? Create videos of the training you can share online. Do a blog post write up of how the sessions went and the key learning points. Training content can be used in so many ways!

The more expert training content you host, the more people will come to realise you're a serious player in your space. Your community will have another valuable arm to it that people feel they need to be a part of.

7. Grow Content Creation

One way to start to grow traffic organically and start to get regular visitors to your community website is to be on top of content creation. The more genuinely useful content you can create, the better your authority in your niche will be, and you just might start to have people coming back to learn more.

There's no quick fix for this step. Creating quality content takes time, but it's a long-term tactic that will massively help you in the long run. Start by doing some research into the kind of topics, discussions and subjects your audience are interested in.

Do some keyword research. Make sure you're targeting helpful long-tail queries of six words or more. And then put content out there regularly. It doesn't have to be loads, but just make sure you are consistent. One high-quality article every two weeks is better than manufacturing four crap articles a week. Speak directly to your audience, to people who have been to your meetups and ask them what would be helpful. What kind of content would they like to see?

8. Secure Paid Community Memberships

Your community is flourishing. You've followed all the above steps, and you've got a strong army of dedicated followers. With any luck (and good old hard work), you've got a website set up that adds a whole lot of value.

The question is, is the information, community feel and training you provide worth paying for? If you put enough time and effort into building a genuinely useful community that your audience feels they HAVE to be a part of, then it's time to secure paid memberships. Get people to pay for access to your content.

However, I must also stress that a lot of communities do well without needing to have paid memberships. It really does depend on your goals and what you want from this. If you're looking to build a business model you can pitch to investors, then securing a decent amount of paid community memberships will add to your appeal. But if you're building a community you want to keep and nourish, it's totally OK to continue to provide useful content and not charge for it. Sometimes pulling the revenue lever slows growth. It's important to consider what you want most at that time?

9. Sales of Business

Congratulations, you've got your community to a point where it's ready to be set free (assuming you're able to let go, that is, you don't have to sell it!). The end goal is to have something that's so enticing to investors that they can't resist. And large communities are worth a lot of money these days. Why? That's a fully engaged audience you've built within a specific niche (worth its weight in gold if you ask me).

If you've done the first eight steps above and want to sell, then you best get prepping. I'm not here to tell you how to pitch to investors (I'm feeling another book incoming!), so I'll leave that part up to you. Congratulations on getting this far. You've achieved Meetup To Millions success.

WHY MEETUPS MATTER?

Your community is waiting for you: waiting for you to bring them together.

Since the beginning of time, the human race has been meeting up in person – to make meaningful connections, to grow authentic relationships and to get support with the things that matter the most.

> *"There is no substitute for getting to know people in person. You can only truly get to understand someone's interests and passions this way. There's no online alternative to being able to see the energy in their eyes and the animation in their body when they are engaging in something that fascinates them."*
>
> —Fiona MacNeill, Ladies That UX Brighton

Would cavemen have evolved properly if they had all their interactions on Zoom? It's certainly food for thought.

But the bottom line is meetups matter, and I'm here to tell you why.

If there's one thing that the 'COVID years' taught us, it is how strong our adaptability to being solely dependent on the virtual world is.

We found new ways to meet and new ways to keep in touch with people that, before, we were seeing each and every single day.

Last-minute briefing? Zoom. Quick team catch-up? Teams. Request from a colleague? Slack. Connecting with a business lead? LinkedIn. Yes – that's brilliant (and honestly, thank goodness we did have these platforms!).

But one thing that none of the online world can provide us with is the deep-rooted human connection that you can only really, truly achieve in person. Remember how you craved seeing others again? How you'd give your left arm for the normality of a buzzy office or work dinner?

In a nutshell, that's why meetups matter: it's the feeling of togetherness and the power of connections. So, if you're brand-new to creating your community, read on because this is the chapter for you.

You've heard the story of Mind The Product's growth, but there are plenty of other amazing community growth stories that came out of the back of smaller meetups.

Take Danny Hope from UX Brighton and Vicky Twomey-Lee of Python, for example. They both began their journeys in a similar way to how Mind The Product did. Think of a small informal meetup.

Danny, the founder of UX Brighton grew his community from a first meetup of a bunch of 60 or so UX enthusiasts to large, extremely successful conferences.

Back in 2004, Vicky found herself at the very first Python Ireland meetup nestled comfortably in a pub. That's where her journey began. There were no platforms like Meetup (launched in 2002 but not big in Europe at that time) or Eventbrite on the market. The crowd had all met organically (yep – word of mouth is a wonderful thing).

The meet-ups began to grow. Vicky took them under her wing by stepping up to volunteer, and with a need for better resources, they began a shiny new conference. PyCon Ireland started in 2010, chaired by Vicky herself and had over 100 attendees from the very beginning.

> *"I learned a lot from being there at the right time... and from the leaders in the community as it was so small and close-knit at the time."*
>
> — Vicky Twomey-Lee

Reflecting on why product people joined Product Tank/MTP to begin with, Guido Lonetti said:

> *"The product management career can be very lonely – typically the set-up is one product manager for 6 to 7 engineers, meaning there was a huge desire for peer support, to share best practices and experiences."*
>
> —Guido Lonetti

That meant that when people found out about ProductTank, it filled a very important gap in the market for a shared product community. One that became a safe space, a place for the sharing of knowledge, a place for product manager therapy!

Guido, Vicky and Danny found a nice little gap in the market to tap into. Having a group of people with a real need to meet and share knowledge is always an effective way to kick things off.

Why Your Community Would LOVE a Meetup

Ready for the magic ingredient to community strength? You're already reading all about it – meetups.

Meetups not only give an individual a place where they can learn and find out more information on specialist topics, but also a place where so many like-minded individuals can come together. Sparks of passion if you will.

Paul Axtell, corporate trainer and author of the book Meetings Matter, described that:

> *"In-person meetings provide a sense of intimacy, connection and empathy that is difficult to replicate via video... It's much easier to ask for attentive listening and presence, which creates the psychological safety that people need to sense in order to engage and participate fully."*
>
> —Paul Axtell, 2015. (Meetings Matter: 8 Powerful Strategies for Remarkable Conversations.)[23]

Along with the above comes peer support. Breathe in, breathe out, and tell us your biggest professional issues – because the more network connections your community has, the more it'll become just like one big therapy session. Yep, we all need our head clearing and problems solved at times.

Professionals (and anyone, for that matter), strive to thrive – they each want to become one of the best-connected experts on a specific topic. That also means you'll get the turnout you want for your meet-up – so relax with the first-timer jitters; you've got this.

The Pros Keep Coming

Strong statement incoming: good connections equal better mental health. Yup. Sharing experiences with other people can be euphoric.

Imagine the glee of winning a sports match with your team or the laughs you share amongst friends at a stand-up comedy night. There's something about having others by your side that makes the little moments so much more... enjoyable.

We had a long-standing saying on the team:

"Something's always on fire, and if you don't know where it is, you haven't looked hard enough!"

It came from the time a US sponsor brought a display unit over to London, forgot the voltage difference, and caused a small plume of smoke in the venue! The crew has a replacement device rented and available in minutes, but the story was one that caused countless laughs in the years that followed.

Working from Home

In the last few years, nearly half of the population have been working-from-home in some capacity, with 16% of those working from home exclusively (stats from 2023)[24]. That's a lot of screen time and lonely desk spaces right there.

In so many cases, we've had our usual 9-5 day at the office ripped away from us, taking our human interaction down with it. We've gone from seeing new faces every single day to faces illuminated on our laptops. That's fine, and it works – but we're hard-wired to need a little more connection at times, and that's what makes meetups an absolute gem, especially now.

Look at juniors and fresh grads, for example. They're now siloed at home, with no wealth of knowledge plonked at the desk next to them, no professionally geared gossip around the water cooler and certainly no post-work networking at the pub.

That's where meetups step onto the scene – a 'home' for compatible relationships, a place to grow and a community to lean on when there's nowhere else to turn.

So go – do it. If you've figured out a niche you want to target, it's time to fill the gap in the market and start your community.

Online vs. Offline

I can already hear your murmurs, *"how come you can't achieve this community strength through online platforms?"*.

I've touched on it previously – and of course, online platforms are an absolute must-have for your community in this day and age. In fact, you can still build communities this way, and meet them too – but there's something special about in-person meetups that just work... Here's why.

Everything's more memorable when you can put a face to the name[25]. And although it may seem obvious, faces are easier to read in person and easier to leave a lasting impression in your memory.

On a similar theme – you, me and the next person all communicate through non-verbal cues[26]. Think: facial expressions, body language, physical contact and laughing. All of this combined gives the recipient added context to the conversation, along with your own thoughts and feelings. As a part of that, it builds strength, rapport and trust (all of the good stuff!). Stronger connections = stronger community.

Have you read What Every BODY is Saying by Joe Navarro? He's a world-leading expert on body language, having spent 25 years in the FBI.

> *"The majority of individuals view their surroundings with a minimal amount of observational effort. They are unaware of the rich tapestry of details that surrounds them, such as the subtle movement of a person's hand or foot that might betray his thoughts or intentions."*
>
> —Joe Navarro, 2008. (What Every BODY is Saying: An Ex-FBI Agent's Guide to Speed-Reading People.) [27]

Another way to grow the strength of a connection is through general chat[28] – getting to know somebody for who they really are – past the business talk. But this type of conversation isn't something that flows effortlessly on a Zoom call, not like an in-person chat can.

Growing rapport and healthy relationships can be a game-changer in the professional world. It means you can tailor how your conversations take place and twist this towards your desired outcome.

Togetherness: It's Human Nature

Mother Theresa once said, *"together we can do great things,"* and that we can. The world is made up of amazing communities, and so has been the case throughout history. Great but not exclusive to the business world – the strength of unity can be applied to every aspect of life.

New mums seek support from other new mums with their new bundles of joy in small meetups at the local village hall; book club members seek inspiration for their next chosen page-turner in the city library; political parties set up for a hot debate on strategies before the next election. It's happening all around us – every day.

Every meet-up provides different things: Learning, camaraderie, therapy, support, a change of scenery, environment, the sheer creativity and brain sparks that come from serendipitous conversations. What will yours offer?

Communities can have an enormous impact on our mental health. Research has consistently found that a strong sense of community belonging is linked to better mental health.

> *"Weaker community belonging exhibited an association with both poorer general and mental health, though a stronger association was observed with mental health."*
>
> —SSM Popul Health, 2020.[29]

When you look at the simple facts, you can see why communities are so important. They help us to feel like we belong and offer opportunities to socialise. And there's a lot of research that shows if you don't socialise and live an isolated life, you don't live as long as people who do socialise!

In 2019 a review of 148 studies found that people who are isolated[30] have a 50% higher risk of premature death than those with stronger social connections. And a 2023 study from the Journal of Epidemiology and Community health discovered that people who socialise occasionally lived longer than those who didn't socialise. And those who socialised every single day lived the longest!!

If you're building a community, make sure it's one where people can touch base and grow new connections. Create community Whatsapp groups, make introductions, give people platforms where they can speak and arrange get-togethers. This will be great for both your community and its members.

The Proof's in the ~~Pudding~~ Success Story

Don't just take my word for it, though – there are so many businesses thriving out there. Why? Because they, too, put their trust in the hands of community meetups.

You've read about Mind The Product – and just to prove we didn't fluke it, I have to introduce you briefly to the story of Danny Hope's UX Brighton, which we will expand upon later in the case studies chapter.

Their origin is almost identical to Mind The Product.

They, too began their journey as a handful of like-minded folks in a place where all great things are born – the pub. Danny began his community building journey as one of the only UX designers in Brighton. He knew that it was hard for industry specialists to get together and chat about all things UX. Their first event was held in 2008 and 60 people attended. Not bad for a first event!

They expanded from this initial meetup, growing with every in-person event that they held. Now, they host events which attract up to 660 people. UX Brighton put a huge emphasis on in-person events. They only host in-person events and really recognise that real life meetups matter!

> *"We're humans and humans are adapted for social interactions. You don't get that online."*

—Danny Hope, UX Brighton

Hang around for the full lowdown on UX Brighton and how it grew to be so successful.

HOW TO HOST YOUR FIRST EVENT

You've decided that hosting a meet-up is the right thing for your community – and although I may be biassed, I think that's a great decision!

Feeling nervous? Maybe unequipped? Have no fear – this chapter's going to give you a handy 101 guide so you can replace the butterflies in your stomach with a sense of thrill and accomplishment!

So, what makes the first event SO important?

The number one (of hopefully many) meet-ups is all about setting the intent and tone of your community. As a group now intertwined, what will your hallmarks be? What are the hopes and dreams of the team you're leading?

The doors close, and your audience are all sat down in their chairs as they look up at you with eagerness, intrigue and optimism glinting in their eyes. It's at this very moment that your community culture will begin to ignite.

What are you going to instil in them? What will your culture be? It's your time to shape it.

Ready for a smooth-flowing meet-up that's completely your own? Here goes...

Are You Going Alone or with Others?

The first thing you'll want to decide is whether you're crafting this in-person community on your own or with others on the same page. There are pros and cons to both – the ball will start rolling a lot quicker when you go solo, but you'll have a quick support network from day one if you're running it with others by your side.

Look for 'guardian' type people to help you launch your community. People who will help safeguard it and shout about its brilliance.

Starting out solo? No worries – you're very likely to discover willing collaborators at your first event, and you can bring them on board with your vision early doors.

Define the Purpose of Your Meet-up

What's the reason for your in-person event, and what are the goals you want to achieve from it? Maybe you're hosting a fundraiser (and so you'll want to go big), maybe you want to bring together a group of people from the same industry (so you can keep it close-knit), or maybe it's to introduce a new concept to a brand-new network.

Whatever it is, having a clear purpose for your meet-up will help you to determine your audience, the structure of the session[31] and (literally) everything else involved in the process. You may even want to classify your event. In 'Event Management' by Lynn Van der Wagen, she talks about Event Classification. The three things that help classify an event are the size, motivation for running the event and the event characteristics. If you drill down into these areas, you'll have a clearer idea of exactly what your event actually is. Van der Wagen says that most events end up being minor events, and that this presents an opportunity for event managers to learn and gain experience. Perfect! That's exactly what you're doing.

Having a defined purpose will also encourage others to come to your session because they'll understand from the get-go how they can professionally or personally benefit from attending.

Another thing to consider is – what's your niche?

> *"We were the first thing of its kind in the world. That's a good place to start. Finding a gap, being ahead of the curve. Be the only people that do that, or the first."*

—Danny Hope, UX Brighton

To spark a level of enthusiasm in all of your attendees, a niche is essential[32]. It ensures that your guests will find value in your meet-up.

> *"Identify your niche and dominate it. And when I say dominate, I just mean work harder than anyone else could possibly work at it."*

—Nate Parker[33]

Go too broad and you risk boring (or not being relevant) to your guests (and that's definitely NOT what you want unless you're promoting a group for insomniacs!). Focus is really beneficial here, like minded people are the aim.

Don't forget, you can ask your community for help! If people value the experience they've had, they will often find ways to help make things better. However, they need to be asked, otherwise they may be shy in coming forward.

By the way, you can create an "Ask stack rank". Wondering what this is? It's a list of things that are important to your community. You can create one with free with a stack ranking tool such as https://www.opinionx.co/[34].

If you get your first meetup right, it's a good idea to be prepared for explosive growth. Organisers should prepare their minds for when they get these things right, their community can grow quickly. Within that community, they will also find the help and support they need!

Choose The Format of Your Meet-Up

Will you be a small group gathered in an informal setting where attendees feel like they can speak above the chatter? Or do you crave the big set-up of a formal hall where a main speaker can talk and be heard across the room?

The format of your meet-up could really be anywhere or anything.[35] For example, once you've got an established community, you can work on your team building in the great outdoors, doing unexpected activities, escape rooms or group sports (who doesn't love a team rounders session!).

The format of your meeting can be determined by the type of person you're inviting. For a brand-new, fresh-faced meet-up, it's probably best to have less structure, where meaningful conversations can flow effortlessly without feeling forced or awkward. But as the group grows and you get a taste of what works and what doesn't, you can tailor this.

Remember, if your group is meeting for the first time, no matter the format, have a few ice-breakers[36] and convo-starters at hand.

Budget!

It's your very first event, so you probably aren't about to roll out the red carpet to the Ritz, but I get it – it's easy to get a little excited when planning your meet-up ('cos hey, you want it to be a success, right!).

So, one of the first steps to consider before planning your step into the world of meet-ups is how much budget you can set aside.[37] Does the venue require payment, or are you keeping it low-key in a local pub? Are you putting on nibbles? (Hint: who doesn't love free beer and snacks?) How are you planning to outreach?

If you can find a company who has a vested interest in the community you're building, they'll often offer to host gatherings for you. Perfect! You'll get the space for free, often with presentation equipment, and may even persuade them to provide some refreshments. In return, offer them the opportunity to say a few words to the audience, but keep it brief, not a heavy sales pitch.

It's your first shot, so I'd expect that you don't need a huge budget for this first event – but it's something to bear in mind.

As your community multiplies and you need bigger, better, fancier venues and possibly payment for guest speakers, then you can offset the costs by charging for tickets to the event or consider sponsorships. More on those later..

To start with though, don't put people off your newbie meet-up by charging. My advice would be to start low-key and let your group organically grow before pulling out the big guns. Or, should I say the red carpet to the Ritz.

Pencil It In

At the risk of coming across as super obvious – set yourself a date in the diary. You want your meet-up to be far away enough that people can make the time to schedule it in, but not too far away that it gets forgotten about. Send invite reminders to remind people!

We would typically look to announce a meetup four to six weeks in advance, and then remind people about it just one week in advance so they could update RSVPs.

Think about your demographic – what date and time would suit them?

Things to consider on date selection: if your attendees all come from a similar group or business, are there any events already ongoing that could clash with yours? Also, what about any major sporting activities or national holidays going on in the same city - these could cause travel delays, so it's one to bear in mind. You'll also want to consider any potential travel issues or disruptions that could occur.

As your community grows, it may be worth recording the sessions and later mailing them out, making each member feel a part of it, even when they can't be there physically. Mind the Product did this really well. Here's a link to a collection[38] of hundreds of recorded videos that community members can view and learn from anytime they want.

What Venue Do You Have in Mind?

We've touched on this briefly when mentioning the format of the meeting – but now it's time to book your venue.[39]

My top tip: Make sure you have plenty of space for everyone on the invite list – too many seats are better than too few.

Do you plan on offering canapes a three-course meal, or is there simply a cash bar for folks to buy their own beverage? This will depend on your audience and whether you're keeping it formal or more casual.

Gatherings can become more formal as they grow. I've been to some with wonderful food and drink on offer. However, the vast majority start out with a much more organic approach, often just reserving a spot at a bar and attendees buying their own drinks.

Ring the venue ahead of time and make sure they can fit you in! Of course, you're going to do this as a standard for big conferences and fancy events, but really, you should do this even with a small casual meet-up in a pub.

You don't want to be caught short wandering the streets of a dismal, rainy city, looking for a new bar to chat in because the one you earmarked is full. Or worse, there's already a party kicking off that's not exactly the right vibe for a business meetup.

This actually happened to one Mind the Product meetup. The members were told to meet at a specific bar, but unfortunately no one called the bar ahead of the event to check availability.

A group of 50 people turned up to find a rather risqué party getting started and had to quickly find a new venue in the rain! It's certainly a memorable funny story, but it wasn't very convenient at the time! We did manage to find another venue just in the nick of time – we moved to a cocktail bar 10 mins walk away and the story went down in local legend.

One of the reasons for working with local organisers in each city, not just running things centrally, is that they'll almost always have alternative venues in mind. You'll also want to consider whether it's easy for all your attendees to get to. Do they all work in a central area? If your community is currently based in a specific area, then why would you choose anywhere else to host your event?

Lastly – remember that budget you created? Make sure you stick to it!

Who Are You Inviting?

Another one of my top tips would be just that – keep it small to start. Events can grow at the speed of light, and when they do, it can be exhilarating. You'll learn so much from the first dinner party!

However, the focus on your first few meet-ups will be what you can take from them – the learnings to be taken.

The smaller the group – the more intimate the group.

That means your audience is more likely to interact and digress into the more personal subjects. It also gives individuals the confidence to stand up and ask their burning questions.

Doing that in bigger groups can feel intimidating! Kreijns et al (2003)[40] established that social interaction is a huge factor in collaborative learning, and as such, a small group can boost this.

Not to think too negatively (because I trust your event will go to plan!), but smaller events also equal fewer things to go wrong and less risk.

Content is King

Now, you've probably got a rough idea of what you'd like to achieve and where the magic will take place, but what will you bring to the table? It's time to start planning.

Content is such a huge thing to consider, the great differentiator! Without content, your community may as well just go for a post-five o'clock catch-up at the pub.

Your content could be music, professional, hands-on, team building, speaker/listener, seminars – you get the gist! It's also important to consider that the content of the event fits with the ethos and values of your audience.

Even for professional events, people love a freebie. You could consider opening with a prize for the speakers, or goodie bags (especially if you're networking with potential clients). Or, hiring out a fun activity to run alongside and get acquaintances to chat (I'm sure you've been charmed by a magician at a networking event before, right? See, you don't forget that kind of event!). Venue is also a great way to make a memorable impact. I bet you remember most rooftop view venues you've visited, and why!

Will your meet-up be a collective of brand-new faces? Break the ice with name tags! It's the simple things that'll really make a difference. If you have name badges for your attendees, this is space a sponsor might like to see their brand on for the evening!

Send Out Your Invites

In a world that's overwhelmingly online, you'll most likely want to send out your invites digitally. But physical ones work just as well. Your preferred method will depend on your type of meet-up and the people you're inviting.

However, you need to think carefully about the safety of your attendees and any data privacy legislation that might apply - GDPR in the UK and Europe, for example.

Whichever way you're inviting people, here are a few things to make sure you put on your invite: the date, the time, the venue, RSVP information and dress code and any security procedures or identification the venue security team might require. Plus, anything exclusive to your event.

If your event has a timeline or schedule – you could include this, too.

Market Your Meet-up

You've sent your invites – and that also means your meet-up is out in the open – being spoken about, being RSVP'd to (hopefully). So, technically, you've already marketed it in a small way.

An easy way to get word of mouth flowing is to further communicate with your target audience, that could be via social media, further emails, or connecting with companies/groups whose members may be interested in further spreading the word. Nigel Jackson stated in his book, Promoting and Marketing Events, that *"the interaction between internal and external audiences is a core part of shaping the final event experience."*[41]

Remember to ask your speakers and sponsors to promote your event too. They have reach you won't, and by sharing your event, all of you win. You might need to make this easy for them by preparing a few choice words and including a link for them to share. If you haven't already, it could be worth making your own website, so when you're talking about the event, you have a simple page to direct people to.

A note on RSVPs and event promotion tools.... Be wary of some platforms charging you unexpected fees. There are plenty of free-to-use options that will work perfectly for your starter event.

Another cautionary tale – some platforms may try to lock in the data you receive from your audience, making it impossible to reach individuals directly or move to other platforms.

Although figuring out what platforms you want to use may be a subject you'll tackle later down the line – it's worth knowing that you have the option to migrate data easily when you need it in the future.

Send a Reminder to Your Guests

Hooray – it's a week until the big day! Now is a great time to send out some reminders to your guests.

Whilst you're at it, it's a good idea to email the venue, plus any speakers, entertainment or caterers that you have booked, to ensure that they're still okay for the date and have you pencilled incorrectly.

If you're planning your event with others, it might be worth checking in with each other at this point, too, just to make sure you're all on the same page and have a rough plan for the day.

Meet, Greet, and Keep Engaged

Like all new things – there's going to be apprehension from your members. Apprehension about whether your event is going to be worth their while. And, just general first-time nerves, especially if the community is brand new to each other.

What I'm trying to get you to envision is any anxieties your attendees may have. This way, you can make a better effort to make sure everybody feels welcomed, on board and ready to make this the pivotal moment: the start of something special.

Remember what I said about ice-breakers? Make sure your small talk game is a class above the rest. Have conversation starters up your sleeve, ready to go. If there is a conversation flowing, it automatically makes everything seem 100% less daunting.

You, yes YOU, are the main string pulling the movement of the puppet (if you like a metaphor). Your attendees came because of you, and it's your job to get people talking, bridge the gaps and connect the links.

Reflect and Learn

Deep breath – you did it!

In the swirl of excitement that comes from bringing a group of people together, there are a few things to consider:

What went well? What could be improved?

Of course, you have your own opinion of how it all went, but there are also another lot of heads who will have different thoughts – so gathering their feedback is invaluable.

Fiona MacNeill from Ladies That UX Brighton said that feedback was critical for them. They'd gather useful feedback and suggestions from attendees, both by carrying out surveys and also anecdotally.

The group wants the events to reflect the interests and trends of the local community. Events are always relevant and stretch beyond the expected.

You can gather feedback with a simple follow-up email to your attendees. Or, you could curate a short survey to get an overall consensus on how your event was received. Guests may be more open and honest on an anonymous survey than simply emailing you some advice.

Now would probably be a good time to ask your guests whether they know anybody else who would be interested in attending next time – you can get their details from them or ask your guests to recommend your events to them. Word of mouth – we love to see it!

Follow-Up

The meet-up itself is just the beginning. The beginning of a beautiful network of people: a community, your community.

The flame has been ignited, but it's up to you to keep it alive. Reach out to your new members regularly and keep them up-to-date with future plans.

Because your future plans are the twisting, turning paths that'll lead you to success.

THE ANATOMY OF A SUCCESSFUL CONFERENCE

If you're aiming to build successful events around the world, you're going to need to know how to put on a brilliant conference. But don't worry, you don't need to go and buy 'conferences for dummies', interview loads of conference directors, or Google 'how to organise a conference' (which gets 50 searches a month in Google, by the way!) – because I've done a deep dive for you. I've mentally gone back to all the conferences and tried to identify key things they all had in common.

You learn a lot from running conferences around the world. Some things go well, some not so well! But you learn quickly. However, I'm here to try and prevent you from making major mistakes and share my most useful conference tips! I've come to discover over the last decade or so that there are seven key parts that must all come together to create the perfect conference. In this chapter, we'll explore the ANATOMY of a successful conference.

The idea is that if you ensure your conference has these key parts, then you'll be on your way to success. I can't guarantee you'll pull it off on the day (I'm not a conference miracle worker!), but you'll put yourself in a really good position to impress your community.

The ANATOMY of a successful conference:

A - Attendee experience

N - Non-negotiables

A - Audience preferences

T - Tried and tested

O - Orators are crucial

M - Meeting place

Y - Your brand matters

A - Attendee Experience

There isn't anything more important than attendee experience. When you're working on the initial framework for your conference, this is where you should start. Because how you make your attendees feel and what they gain from attending holds the key to your long-term success.

If you make them happy, they'll come back. It's that simple. Make sure everyone comes away feeling like they've gained something from the experience, and you're set. Then you'll have no problem attracting speaker and sponsor interest for future events.

You want to deliver an experience they will remember. Make it memorable. One way to do this? Immersive experiences and some form of entertainment for attendees. A study about immersive event experiences by the University of Greenwich[42] showed that "*that novelty and entertainment are highly important to attendee motivation.*"

Naturally, food and drink can often have a significant impact on attendee experience. A conference full of hungry people is never going to go down well! And people tend to be at ease and content when they've got access to decent beverage options (whether that's coffee, soft drinks, alcohol etc.)

> *"Food functions, in particular, can be an effective tool to satisfy attendees and build attendance, as it empowers an attendee's sensory memory of an event. Nutritiously balanced food can enhance an attendee's learning ability."*

—A case study by Yen-Soon Kim, Yoon-Young Lee & Curtis Love.[43]

One year, we'd tested the lunches at the venue beforehand, and decided on their bento box option. This allowed people to collect food quickly, then sit with other attendees as they wished and keep talking. On the day, the boxes provided were actually so much smaller than those we'd tested. Many attendees took double, meaning we had nowhere near enough to go around.

> *"The quality of food content is the leading determinant of an attendee's satisfaction with the food function performance and that food function predicts an attendee's intention to return. This research provides insights into how important food functions are to conference attendees' intent to return to future conferences."*

—A case study by Yen-Soon Kim, Yoon-Young Lee & Curtis Love.[44]

We had to do some serious damage control! Thankfully our team rose to the challenge. We rallied the volunteer crew to scour every sandwich shop locally and bring back trays to feed the hungry. It was a very noticeable hiccup, for which we immediately apologised on stage as the afternoon session started.

After the event, we went further. We obtained a refund on the catering from the venue, then put that credit onto a series of gift cards. We emailed all attendees from that event and invited them to let us know if they hadn't been satisfactorily fed that day. *"Your ticket was supposed to include lunch, and we failed you. Let us know if this was you, and we'll send you a gift card so you can at least go and get lunch on us now!"*.

The audience showed us so much love for this after the event, and it just reinforced the loyalty we'd been building all along. Mistakes can happen. Venues can let you down. If you underdeliver, go above and beyond to fix it and people will likely be understanding. When a conference screws up, it will be noticeable, and the audience may call it out. Own it, apologise, and tell them how you'll ensure it's better next time.

N - Non-negotiables

What do I mean by non-negotiables in relation to running a conference? The things you feel your conference won't work without. You need to be clear on these things from the outset. Why? Well, you don't want to get to a week before the big day and realise you've really not nailed the basics. Then it's a huge scramble to get everything right, and that's no fun for anyone involved. With our Mind The Product Conferences, our non-negotiable/curation rules were...

1. How speaker decisions would be made:

For example, no all-male line-ups.

2. Our attendee experience standards:

Things like coffee & lunch included, solid wifi.

3. The role we wanted sponsors to play:

Where they would be visible, and where they would not! For example, no sales people on stage, ever!

4. What we would and what not do with attendee data:

For example, sponsors could scan a badge with our permission to connect, but we would NOT share personal information with them otherwise - and several would ask each year if they could buy the mailing list. Hard no!

A - Audience Preferences

You don't ask, you don't know. If you're running a conference, I'd live by this saying. If you've not asked your audience what they want, how do you know you're serving up things that are relevant to them? Don't make the mistake of assuming they may want something a certain way over another. Why? Because you could end up getting it completely wrong and hurting your reputation and growth potential in the process.

When it comes to conferences, the little things can truly have a big impact. And yes, this really can come down to seemingly minute things like their coffee preferences.

So it's worth gathering data on your audience as a whole and considering what their wants and needs may be. As well as studying this data, spend time imagining being in their shoes, walking through your conference venue doors. Is there anything you know your community would need?

For example, with Mind the Product, we had an audience of folks who work in tech, so we tested hard on venue wifi and made sure there was a good cloakroom facility for people wanting to drop laptop bags. We knew that our audience really appreciated decent coffee, so we persuaded a sponsor to foot the bill for a barista coffee cart, and people could have whatever coffee they wanted, not just the usual conference centre brown water!

And as mentioned above, making assumptions can lead to you barking up the wrong tree. Here's a handy MTP example to illustrate this. When we decided to launch a paid membership programme to help us survive COVID, one of the first things we needed to figure out was what might be included.

We looked at other paid membership content and saw things ranging from VIP events to private premium content, exclusive training offerings, early access to tickets, and even deep discounting.

We initially assumed that ticket discounting might be one of the first things people wanted, but we knew we should test that assumption. We conducted a stack ranking exercise - where you list out the possible things you might be, then ask people to rank them in order of importance.

What we learned from this blew our assumptions away and massively influenced the final shape of the programme. For example, that ticket discounting? No one cared! In fact, it was actually at the bottom of the list. It was all being expensed back to their employer anyway, so they were far more interested in things like regular sessions where we'd invite an industry legend to come and participate in an online A&S session. If we hadn't tested those assumptions, we might have discounted needlessly!

T - Tried and Tested AND Surprise

When things work, there's a reason for it. There are loads of examples of successful conferences and communities around the world. We've touched on a few of them in this book. Case studies line up for you to, well, study.

There's so much value to be gained from looking at popular conferences and the elements that made them work. Look at other successful conferences in your niche. You can even start with what you know about yourselves.... making a list of things you dislike about other conferences. That gives you a great starting point on what to cut, and what to invest in!

Whenever you make big decisions, it's a good idea to go with tried and tested things that you know work. Particularly when you're just starting out and running your first conference. You can always experiment and innovate as your conference brand grows and you've got an established audience.

According to globalconference.ca[45], the four features of a successful conference are:

- Interactive activities
- Suitable venue
- No major technical issues
- Good food

These are the absolute basics, but getting these things right has clearly worked for a lot of other conferences. Look to the market to see what's working, and then do it better than all your competitors!

Research on how different surprising outcomes affect memorability differentially found that *highly surprising events are more memorable.* Research by Meadhbh I. Foster and Mark T. Keane[46] showed, *"surprise scenarios bear a complex relationship to memorability. Less-known surprises were remembered more accurately than known surprises."*

Why? Because people remember surprises, and big unexpected surprises are more memorable. In the context of a conference, if you surprise them by throwing in an unexpected experience, they're more likely to remember it. It will be the thing they leave talking about.

> *"To elevate a moment, do three things: First, boost sensory appeal. Second, raise the stakes. Third, break the script."*

—Chip and Dan Heath (The Power of Moments)[47]

Let's break that down for your conference into a doable scenario:

- Elevate the moment- Bring in an unexpected guest or form of entertainment.
- Raise the stakes - Offer an audience member the chance to win something.
- Break the script - End the performance with audience members being able to have a go too, which is something they may not have expected.

Give your audience something to talk about when they leave. The moments you create on the day are so important. This is a sure-fire way to get your conference to be more memorable than all the rest!

O - Orators (Speakers) are Crucial

What's the one major thing that's going to entice people to your conference? Decent speakers. You need more than just your average Joe. You need to secure industry-leading figures. Names that will draw people in. If you want to give up-and-coming speakers a shot, that's fine (I'm all for that); just make sure you've got one or two big names.

We've had a whole host of inspiring speakers at the MTP conferences. We were in the Product Management space -

the acknowledged godfather of the modern discipline is Marty Cagan, and we were delighted that he accepted our invitation to come to the very first London conference. It really put us on the map immediately as highly credible.

Over the years, we hosted speakers from Google, Spotify, Microsoft and so many other household-name tech firms. Often, it wasn't the speaker name that was the big seller, it was that we offered you the chance to hear from someone who'd built a product you really respected.

A huge one for us was seeing sales pitches on stage, so curation became a core part! We needed speakers from both large and small firms, speakers from the US and Europe, we wanted to show great diversity. Mapping all these things out at the start really helped.

We constantly see conferences in tech just putting up a list of speakers from the same demographic. The tech events world has a deservedly bad name for the lack of gender equality on stage, and events often get called out for this.

With Mind the Product, Martin achieved equality on every keynote stage we delivered, a rarity in the industry. We didn't shout about this enough at the time. Representation matters! It wasn't easy to deliver that, but the whole team kept a watch to contribute new speakers we might want to give that spotlight to in future. The meetup organisers around the world acted as talent spotters.

Beyond that, on a regular basis we would spot an upcoming speaker that had a great story but maybe wasn't ready for the main stage - and we'd offer them speaker coaching. We committed hard to changing the balance, and it made a real difference.

M - Meeting Place (venue)

Let's be completely real here, if you don't pick the right venues, your conference will fall flat. This is no doubt one of the most important decisions. When it comes to venues, there are so many things to consider.[48] From the cost and size capacity to layout, aesthetics, and practical things like parking. You need to spend a fair amount of time identifying what your audience needs from a venue. For example, will they want meeting room facilities? Research shows that *"meeting organisers find meeting room facilities to be a critical factor in venue choice."*[49]

Successful conferences get the venue right. They choose a venue that meets the exact needs of their audience and keeps things hassle-free on the day. You need to identify things that will impress your attendees, but it's also worth making a note of what you think will turn them off. Or ask them directly. For example, if the venue doesn't hit certain sustainability credentials, will your audience be put off attending?

Always consider the practicalities and the comfort of attendees. A really cool venue may seem like a way to stand out, but does it deliver on the basics? Does it have a suitable space where people can meet and feel comfortable?

There are many conferences held in uber-cool warehouse buildings or old breweries. While that feels very real and connected with the City it's in, you often end up with awkward stage views, uncomfortable seating, etc. Since our roots were in meetups hosted in bars or co-working spaces, we decided we wanted a very different experience for the conference. The meetups would be free to attend, hosted in a variety of locations, and with a scrappy, organic vibe to them.

For the conferences, we wanted to lean into the other end of the scale. Attendees would buy tickets to attend, and that would give them the right to expect more. We balanced our budgets carefully, and decided to aim for the kind of venues that would normally host orchestras or other arts performances! Beautiful spaces, great acoustics, comfortable seating. It meant we needed to upgrade the audio-visual kit or wifi sometimes, but it was important to us that the conferences represented the pinnacle of the Mind the Product experience.

Y - Your Brand Matters

You can do all the right things, put on a great conference, and make people happy – but if your branding is 'meh' then you'll struggle to really take off. As with any kind of business, it's worth investing time and money in your branding.

Don't plan your whole conference and then think, 'holy crap, we better pull some branding together!' You need to get your branding sorted before you get into all the planning stages. This helps you to have a clear vision from the get-go, and it also shows prospective speakers, attendees, and sponsors that you mean business. You want your brand to be instantly recognisable and memorable.

Mind the Product always had a strong visual identity, centred on the cyan Venn logo still widely visible across the web. Prior to the San Francisco conference one year, we ran a social event for the volunteer crew the evening before so they could get to know one another. We had branded t-shirts on so our volunteers could find us easily.

Totally at random, a Product Manager from Facebook HQ walked in. He recognised the logo and introduced himself, so pleased to be meeting the folks from a business he loved!

He went further, and mentioned he had an event operations friend in London looking for a new role! He introduced us to him, and Marcus was hired not long after. He became one of the absolute stars of our crew! He was hired via a chance meeting in a bar thousands of miles from home, by virtue of our strong brand doing the work for us. Never underestimate the power of branding.

And that's it. That's the ANATOMY of a successful conference, from the MTP perspective anyway. Follow these key parts, and you'll be able to put your best (conference) foot forward. Now go on, put it into action. I'm looking forward to hearing all your success stories!

CREATING MEMORABLE MOMENTS

Make It Extraordinary; Make It Unforgettable

When's your earliest memory? Age 4? 5? What was that memory? It can literally be anything. Mine's the smell of stables of all things! I grew up in the countryside and used to walk the family dog with my parents constantly. I remember being astonished the first time I saw horses up close and personal (HUGE DOGS!) and the smell was overpowering.

Typically the moments we remember more readily are connected with emotions, and studies like that from Stenson et al. (2019) show that emotion typically enhances memory.[70]

So, as you cast your mind back, you'll probably find that your most memorable moments are the highest of the high or (hopefully not, but we've all had first-love heartbreaks!) the lowest of the low.

You're by now probably questioning why I'm picking at your memories. But it's all in the name of perfecting your event management skills. Because this chapter's all about how you can catapult your meet-up into the deep, ingrained memories of every brain that attends your event.

It may not make their core memory bank (I'd be super impressed if your event managed that), but hopefully they'll form a strong memory in their mind of what they experienced.

> *"Memory can change the shape of a room; it can change the colour of a car. And memories can be distorted. They're just an interpretation."*

—Leonard, first act from the film 'Memento'.

Extraordinary events make unforgettable stories that'll last a lifetime. And if your event is vibrant and engaging enough, people will remember them in their own unique way.

Of course, there's no secret formula to success, but there are a whole host of things to consider when planning your meet-up that will then put you in the right direction.

Who's Coming?

Let's begin with your invitees.

We've touched on this before, but it's SO important that you're inviting the right people.

If your audience has an interest in the subject, then they're going to pay more attention and ultimately remember more from the date. Sounds so simple, right?

Also, consider getting a broad spectrum of attendees - ones that'll mix, mingle, and chat. This means you'll probably want to reach out to more than just a few colleagues who already know each other.

Networking events are amazing for sparking new and exciting conversations. So, as long as your group has that one thing in common, you can go quite diverse with whom to invite.

The conversation is key. In fact, studies have shown that *"the higher the level of participants' social interaction... the better [people's] cognitive functioning"*.[71] And therefore, making your event even more significant in their mind.

There's only so much you can do to encourage interaction at your event. But, with a diverse and interested set of people, you'll be on the right track.

Little things to help out? If your attendees are newbies to one another, then have some convo-starters up your sleeve. Or, for bigger events, sit dynamic groups together and give them a talking point. Consider neurodiversity too, and think about whether you'll need quieter spaces, or maybe screen captions for the hard of hearing. Much depends on the audience you attract..

Invitees aren't just the people on the guest list, though - it's your speakers too - actually, just about anybody, entertainers included, who can bring a positive addition to the room.

Vicky Twomey-Lee took on the role of chair in her community (PyCon) because it connected her with the grassroots community, sponsors and companies. She was able to begin building relations with speakers and people that would become vital to the growth of PyConIE. Who you choose as speakers can have a direct impact on the success of your community.

It's important to find engaging guest speakers that will captivate your audience and also resonate with them. Maybe you've already attended an event that had a speaker you thought brought a stand-out speech, or maybe you've got friends, colleagues, industry specialists, or inspiring talkers on your must-invite list.

Whoever you've got earmarked, it's probably worth doing your research on them. Have they spoken at events before? Have they got demo videos online that you can preview before you book them in? Do they fit with the vibe of your meet-up? Will they add value to your event?

More importantly - will their words be remembered?

Location, Location, Location

You've nailed the guest list - but where are you hosting everyone?

Let's cast our minds back once again and think about the key moments in our lifetime. What stands out in your mind? Maybe a sun-soaked holiday in the tropics? Maybe it's dancing the night away at a loved one's wedding? Maybe it's the simplicity of the smiles a family day out at the zoo brought!

One thing is for sure (and please correct me if I'm wrong!), but when I just asked you to think of a stand-out moment, your mind certainly didn't just take you to a random gloomy Tuesday in April where life rolled by as usual.

Very often, we're consumed by the mundane every day. The 6 am alarm ringing in our ears, the journey to the office, the same building, the same desk, the same commute home.

When we eat, work, sleep, repeat (even when we enjoy it!), it becomes a part of the every day: it doesn't stand out.

So how do we make a normal day extraordinary?

When your mind takes you down memory lane, the visions it evokes and the places you think of are most likely set somewhere special.

The place we call home, the place we love spending time or a place that's new, intriguing, and exciting. Buchanan (2008)[72] backs this up by saying, *"Emotional events are often remembered with greater accuracy and vividness".*

So, when you want to make an event stand out. Choose a standout venue.

An Example:

When I was at Mind The Product, we once hired a 65 ft catamaran and took an exclusive group of speakers and sponsors sailing on the San Francisco Bay. Glimmering waters, wind sweeping through our hair, and delicious light refreshments. Who could ask for better?

"Expensive though", I hear you mutter, but actually, it worked out cheaper than a full-service private dining room and I can bet your bottom dollar that the environment we created sits strongly in all the attendee's memory.

I'd love to claim credit for the passing by of a magnificent humpback whale that graced our presence and swam alongside, but I have to admit, that was beyond even our control. (Although, maybe he'd heard about how great our events are!).

Another fine example would be the Slush event in Helsinki. I was invited as part of a group and we all departed for drinks at a health spa. Here we settled into a stunning retreat and were provided with everything we needed to relax and unwind in the saunas.

For an extra adrenaline rush, we were all encouraged to jump into the freezing November Baltic waters (because you can't waste the opportunity of your surroundings!), before racing back into the sauna to warm up again.

And that's the kind of setting that conjures up happy memories. These go well beyond meet up events - but we started with a single meetup and ended up with a 65 ft Catamaran. How far do you want to go?

A Fitting Ambience

Next up, and going hand in hand with your venue choice, is the ambience of your setting. Did you want to create a calming environment? A classy experience?

You can transform your venue easily with some subtle additions like lighting, decorations that fit the theme and background music. Psst... no one likes the bright, interrogation-like brightness of fluorescent lighting.

It's agreed, with research backing, that *"memorable experience needs to engage all five human senses"*.[73] So, although it seems simple, think of how you can make the event extraordinary in all five senses: sight, sound, taste, touch, and smell.

The Little Details

There's power in the little things. Your aim here is to surprise and delight.[74] To leave a lasting impression on everybody who attends.

This really could be anything: From fancy, bespoke invites that command attention from the get-go all the way to personalised goodie bags to say thank you. For example, I was recently attending an after-party; the organiser had water stations everywhere. That meant zero queuing for the bar when you needed to quench your thirst and regular refreshments on hand at every angle. It also made for a more responsible atmosphere too! Makes it more inclusive as less alcohol often makes women feel safer.

We touched on the element of surprise in chapter 6. But just to remind you, the moments people have at your event really matter.

> *"The 'occasionally remarkable' moments shouldn't be left to chance! They should be planned for, invested in. They are peaks that should be built. And if we fail to do that, look at what we're left with: mostly forgettable.*
>
> —Chip Heath and Dan Heath (The Power of Moments)[75]

Remember - you want to make a big impact, but make sure it's still relevant to what you want to achieve. Always strike the balance between surprise and subject matter.[76] Yep - your event will probably get remembered if you have a bunch of circus entertainers swinging from the ceiling, but they probably won't remember the reason WHY they were there. So, make it relevant.

The No-Nos

To excel, you need to know what NOT to do. And I'll admit not everything was perfect with MTP. Building a community involves a steep learning curve, but I can help you avoid some simple mistakes.

We launched with Meetup[77], as many such informal events do - it was fast and light and helped people find us. As a platform though, we found ourselves limited by it, and unable to get the data out to move elsewhere. Hostages, effectively, and we struggled with that for years. We failed to understand that platform's lack of ambition.

I've taken the below snippet from Phil Mershon's book Unforgettable, The Art & Science of Creating Memorable Experiences because it does an amazing job of summing up the key turn-offs.

*"**What Makes an Event Boring**...*

- *Unprepared, unengaging, or uninspiring speakers*
- *Bad food*
- *Poor organisation*
- *Passive participation*
- *Lack of awareness of time*
- *Too much sitting still*
- *No coffee, or Wi-Fi, or no power chargers*
- *Inauthentic or fake fun*
- *Forced or awkward networking*
- *Long presentations and too much selling*
- *Too much information, not enough insights..."*

There's a lot to take from that list - because if you flip it on its head, it gives you a good place to start!

Another snippet of advice from me is to take the focus off of alcohol. Yes, having a pint or glass of vino on hand is great but realistically, people can get drinks wherever and whenever they want.

They can meet their friends for post-5 o'clock drinks or slip back into the comfort of their own home. It doesn't make your event any more attendable or memorable (in fact it could do the opposite if you were planning on having a free bar!). Instead, lean harder into connecting others together, because there's no substitute for meaningful, human connections.

Your niche is what will bring your event to life. The people are coming because they can only get that "something special" in the environment you've created.

Think about that. If they can get an experience from somewhere else, what makes your meet-up any different?

Tick tock - hear that? The last of your attendees sit on their chairs, the door closes... the clock is ticking. You've got an hour, maybe two if you're lucky, maybe less, to create impact and memories. Make every moment count.

- Pick your attendees carefully - you're aiming for fruitful conversations and limitless mingling!
- Your venue should leave a lasting impression. Think out of the box if you really want something extraordinary.
- Surprise and delight! Make an effort with the smaller details and your guests will appreciate that.

HOW TO MAINTAIN ENGAGEMENT

Wow – what a whirlwind! You've achieved a faultless first event; well done. But before you put up your feet, it's time to follow up.

So soon? I hear you mumble.

Yes! You've got the momentum going – your event is still fresh and forefront of everybody's mind, and there's no better time to maintain a strong engagement.

You've now got a secret weapon. Your soldiers are in place. Wondering what I'm on about? Your first attendees of course. These are the OG's and they're likely to turn into your brand ambassadors. Well, that's if you did your first event right!

And let's just say holding your attendees close is a hell of a lot easier than recruiting new ones.

Engagement is a key attribute of a successful community – one filled with people who attend each and every event. And luckily, I'm here to walk you through how you too can make sure you maintain the closest-knit involvement from each and every member.

A Sense of Togetherness

We've spoken about it in previous chapters, but the most important links in a community are the ones that will seamlessly fuse between each member.

If you can get each individual to come together, it makes the community stronger. The best part about people coming together? You'll have a better chance of retention through strength in numbers.

Think about it this way – imagine you've just been invited to an old friend's birthday party. You don't have a lot to do with them anymore, and quite frankly, you wouldn't be too disheartened about missing out. But a close friend of yours has also been invited. The FOMO kicks in. You have a change of heart. You're intrigued and want to see why your friend is so pumped to go.

Friendships within a community work the same way. In fact, a report by Marketing General showed that 57% of people first joined an association with the sole purpose of connecting with peers.

Peer support is an amazing thing!

Suddenly there's another reason to attend – there's someone to catch up with, someone with things in common, a friendly face to see: there's emotion.

The below comes from Alon Alroy, Eran Ben-Shushan, Boaz Katz's book, Event Success:

> *"Members need to feel an emotional connection to their fellow members. This tends to happen naturally once a community reaches critical mass,*

> *but when it comes to building a foundation, nothing beats a shared emotional experience.”* [78]

As the founder of the event, creating the foundations is in your hands.

There are things you can do to encourage connections.

First and foremost is creating an event where people experience and live the same shared can’t-miss moments, as well as delivering exclusive, can’t-find-anywhere-else content.

This will form bonds between each member and also encourage conversation.

Alongside this, delivering surprising, unexpected and engaging content means your guests will be waiting on tenterhooks for your next big surprise at the next event.

Make Sure the Conversation Never Ends

> *“Social media is all about networking; it is about sharing and discussing information among people via internet-based tools and online platforms. It is where users can share their opinions, content and views using highly accessible publishing techniques.”*

—Strategic Uses of Social Media for Improved Customer Retention by Alsmadi Et Al (2016). [79]

And that is why social media will be a key tool to keep ticking away in the background of your events.

The Role of Social Media in Event Promotion: Expanding Horizons and Engaging Audiences[80] — a home where attendees can express their gratitude and provide feedback in a less formal environment.

Not only is it a great way for your community members to keep in touch, but it's a perfect (and free!) way to advertise your upcoming events. And although it may be tempting to use it as one big advertisement, here's a last note on social media to consider, eloquently put by Cheryll Kimball in Start Your Own Event Planning Business:

> *"Remember, social media provides you with the opportunity to meet your audience – not sell to your audience. People do not join these social media networks to find marketers. They join and participate for friendly interaction and the value that interaction adds to their day. Provide that interaction and you will watch your audience grow."* [81]

Other Platforms

Exposure, exposure, exposure.

Don't just stop at social media sites! Another great way to make sure your members are fully submerged in your world is through regular updates.

How? With E-newsletters that are finely tuned to deliver value to every member.

A study by Jackson (2008)[82] highlighted the influence that newsletters can have on people. His study showed that receiving an MP's e-newsletter had an effect on subscribers' voting behaviour at the 2005 General Election.

Although you're probably not running to be the next political leader, it goes to show how an engaging and relevant newsletter will engage and persuade your community, with the hope they stay loyal members and attendees of your events.

> *"First your database needs to have the correct people on it, and you must continually manage and update it. This means that you need to note how subscribers respond to the e-newsletter and what impact it might have on their relationship with your event... Second, you should have something interesting to say that adds value. Do not just promote your events, but have stimulating stories: the reader of an e-newsletter is looking to get material, such as offers, that they cannot get elsewhere."*
>
> —Nigel Jackson (Promoting and Marketing Events) [83]

Engagement can also fall off a cliff when people forget what a good time they had or what good things they learned. So, rounding all of this up into post-event catch-up follow-up emails is a quick and easy win to remind attendees of the value they uncovered and drive higher future engagement.

Get Organised!

The trouble right now is that there's no single platform that seamlessly combines content sharing, social discussions, insights and newsletters in one handy space.

We struggled with this at Mind The Product – it meant there had to be fine organisation and execution, plus a willingness to tool stack and become well-acquainted with Excel.

It's why I'm now building Rodeo. I know I know – I can barely wait either.

Adapting to Setbacks

Setbacks are a part of the process. They will happen at some point in your journey. It's how you approach them that matters. Many things can slow your momentum: the market, world events, investment issues and even the weather! Our biggest challenge came when the pandemic hit.

COVID and the Move to Membership

The pandemic was a huge blow to us. I mean, we specialised in in-person events. It couldn't have come at a worse time. The meetups were in over 200 cities by this time, the conferences in London, SF, Hamburg, Manchester and we'd even just run our first in Singapore. We also had an extensive training business. We were not only running the workshops in conjunction with the conferences – but also on request, we would go to companies and deliver corporate training for them, which was a wonderful revenue stream to open up.

Everything stopped overnight in March 2020, and our first fear was whether we'd even be able to pay the team. No one wants to be in this position.

The various government schemes did provide some help here, but we knew it wouldn't be enough. The team worked hard and fast to evaluate how we might actually stay in the game. The first analysis was around what assets we had: a global audience who respected our work, and an amazing library of content from all those conference videos, blog posts and more.

The online training courses got some really great early feedback, but the conferences were still an issue as we battled the pandemic. We decided to continue running them online, as a lot of people did at that point. We wondered if there was more that could be done. Something Martin had wanted to do for a while was to look into the backlog of amazing content that we had and see if anything more could be done with that.

We moved quickly to explore what a paid membership model for access to that content might look like.

We looked at it in detail, did some very quick discovery conversations with loyal members of the community (always ask their opinion on major decisions like this), and quickly decided that we could approach the community. The messaging would be something like:

"We've been generating an abundance of amazing content for the last ten years via our online platform. Unfortunately, we can't keep doing this for free during COVID, as we're not able to run the regular conference business. Previously, the conference revenue has subsidised our online community. What we're going to do is create a subscribe premium, subscription service. We're going to ask you to subscribe for a relatively small amount to access that great content. We'll polish the experience, we'll make it better than ever and find new things to offer you. In doing so, you'll help support us to keep doing what we all love and keep the lights on during this difficult period."

We ended up with a fast pivot. We launched that new service in about six weeks! We only had one full time developer on the team to build software, Shaun, who put in a real shift! He worked tight with Martin and Emily to get things out there as fast as we could.

Within about six weeks, we had the first few thousand paying customers on board. It was never going to be the kind of money that you could retire on, but it was enough to help us keep the lights on during that period and that was our primary objective – survival. Sometimes you've just got to push through these dark times and focus on keeping your community alive. And we did that, we managed it, against all the odds.

We had to learn fast. We'd never been a subscription membership business. It was a new area for us and it was tough. We had some great product thinkers on the team who really understood how to do research and how to learn fast. These people absolutely saved our bacon during that period and led to the evolution and development of many more things.

Namrata's Women In Product UK community recently launched a paid membership subscription. Interestingly, the majority of paid subscribers opt for the higher priced package which is a very interesting user behaviour as typically people go for lower priced packages for subscription products.

> *"My marketing spend is zero, I don't have any sales team either. It's 100% word of mouth and referrals. When acquisition and engagement are solid, retention (hopefully) should be solid too, but we'll know that in a year's time. I think the secret sauce here is no secret at all, it simply is the value to the customer! People join*

communities to broaden their network and learn new things, but the ultimate goal for most people is to secure better jobs/opportunities and boost their career growth. When I designed the paid subscription packages, I always thought of the outcome first, and then worked backwards. Ask the question to yourself - why should I pay for this? What will I get out of this? What is the return on investment (ROI)? Of course, the events and content quality has to be top notch; the people in the community have to be top notch too. As a Founder, I'm obsessed about the value to the customer. I'd like our members to land bigger & better roles because of Women in Product UK."

—Namrata Sarmah, Women in Product UK

It's clear that communities reach a point where a paid subscription model makes sense, but getting the timing right is crucial. With Mind The Product, it was a no-brainer when COVID hit and offering an exclusive membership business was an excellent alternative when in-person events were a no-go.

With the membership business alive, we started to look into what else we could do with it and concluded that training was a natural fit. Could we offer people self-directed learning to be completed on their own time, instead of having them attend classes with a raft of other people? And that emerged quite quickly and became a compelling part of the offering.

Having Product thinkers like Martin and Emily at the core of the team proved to be essential. We were also able to take this problem to the community: *"We need to find the ways to keep the lights on during the pandemic, so we'd value your input as we research a new business model"*. Our loyal community was happy to provide ideas and feedback which helped us find the right solution faster.

The workshops moved swiftly to Zoom and we actually found a lot of customers preferred this style. It was less aggravating for them to get everyone in the same location. Online was easy for all attendees, and no cost compared to the expense of booking rooms at HQ or even booking workshop facilities for those clients who didn't have spaces. It was easier for us to schedule the most appropriate trainer from anywhere in a compatible time zone too. This resulted in us having a much wider choice of facilitators.

However, over time as the world recovered from COVID and people started socialising again, it became clear that there was a real need for face to face events. There are many advantages to hosting things online but you lose some of the value of personal relationships that can only truly flourish in the flesh!

There will no doubt be setbacks, particularly when you're trying to grow a large community that may involve in-person events. But the communities that survive are headed up by people who are ready to switch things up should the unexpected happen. You have to be prepared to do this. To pivot. To adapt. And to survive whatever is thrown at you.

Community Data

Until there's a platform that can do it all, you may have to get smart on email analytics and post-event follow-ups. It's not hard to gather feedback – it's just time-consuming.

However, it's invaluable.

Analyse your attendees' behaviours to work out what they are enjoying. What topics do people really engage with? What content sparks attention? What format and experts are your members loving?

Your post-event strategy should always include getting feedback. But be free to experiment with what might get the best responses. Maybe it's a conversation on the night, maybe an email the next day? There is no perfect answer for all shapes of community. It doesn't matter if you're only a few events in or have done 100 before, it's still the best way to give your community a voice.

So, ask for feedback. Send out surveys. Request testimonials. Need advice? Seek it!

After a few events you should have plenty of data to begin segmenting your audience and find what piques their interests. If you want to get really personal, you can boost engagement and community retention by grouping similar groups and targeting them separately.

Brand Ambassadors

Want to keep your community engaged? One way to ensure this happens is to get yourself a group brand ambassadors. People who live and breathe your industry, who are passionate about building a community. If you set up a community that genuinely adds value from the get go, you shouldn't have too much trouble attracting brand champions. With a lot of successful communities, the development of brand ambassadors happened naturally.

Namrata's Women in Product UK is a great example of this. Her members love the community, and they're so invested and passionate that they bring in more members.

She created a founding member group of around 30 people who were evangelists of the brand. They helped to spread the voice of women in product and strengthen the name and the brand. They strongly believed in the value of belonging. Belonging to a community where people feel valued, can seek help from experts and can share ideas with like-minded people.

We had a similar experience with MTP. As the ProductTank community developed in each City, every time we'd find a small handful of people emerging who brought more energy than any other attendee. They wanted to speak, or help host, or support in any other way they could.

We welcomed these folk with open arms, spent hours chatting with them about the aims of ProductTank, about how they might play a supporting role, and what ProductTank might offer them in future. These ambassador roles were never formalised, but many went on to become speakers or even ProductTank organisers themselves. The inner circle kept growing, each addition making the movement stronger than before. We took care to ensure they had a good view of what we felt the community should offer to everyone, and they carried that message with them. So the key thing to keep in mind here is, you need to try and pinpoint any potential ambassadors and foster those relationships. Give these people the information and support they need to spread the word.

Talking about the community's growth – Guido Lonetti (Organiser of ProductTank) expresses that two of the biggest factors were word of mouth and the calibre of the people that attended.

An infectious spirit meant that the people who first just came to link arms with other product professionals then became ambassadors for ProductTank and began asking to organise their own. That equals growth on growth.

The Personal Touch

It's in your hands.

The plan for your events, the environment you're going to offer, the vibe of your community.

And what makes a better host than one who can be accessible at all times, one that's available at the end of a meet-up for a quick heart-to-heart, one that can ping off a quick Whatsapp to a burning question?

Remember a good host is the cornerstone of a good community.

The What-Not-To-Dos

Okay, so I've rounded up the important practices you can slot into your post-event strategy. But what should you avoid?

A big killer is inappropriate and badly considered advertising. It has its place, but be mindful.

Of course, sometimes it's necessary to cover overheads. But once some people get a taste of the financial value of advertising, they go too far. Feedback is your friend!

Remember – your community wants value – not consumer-driven products thrown at them.

Another no-no: Ghosting your community.

Any blog strategist will tell you consistency is key to traffic.

Your audience and/or community lean into baseline expectations.

For example, if you say you'll publish every Tuesday, you should be living up to that! One of the longest and most successful meetups in London made a clear statement: *"We do every third Wednesday evening,"* and as if by magic, the community learned to expect it, to build it into their own strategies and even began booking office days to fit it in.

On one occasion, we had a sponsor who we were looking to hire. Through audience feedback, we found they had a reputation for unethical financial practices, and the community weren't impressed with the association.

We never invited them back, and we learned to evaluate sponsor reputations more closely in future. We also had the occasional sponsor who was overzealous in their pitch or follow up. Again, the community reacted badly.

We developed our practices here to provide guidance to the sponsors in advance on how best to engage and what the community expected. Everyone developed a more nuanced understanding of the expected dynamic.

COMMUNITY CASE STUDIES

Need the proof that Mind The Product wasn't a fluke? That YOU, too, can create an empowered community? There are tons of examples out there.

To give you an occasional break from the MTP journey and show a diverse selection of community examples, I've spoken to several successful community founders. Their stories will be touched upon throughout the book to provide context and explain what does work, and what doesn't!

There are so many brilliant meet-ups happening all over the world. Probably, right at this very second. It's so useful to be able to gain first hand advice from people who have been there and done it. They've not only given me an insight into how they got to where they are, but they've each given me their top feedback for creating, growing and leading communities.

To avoid confusion and prevent you from wondering who and what I'm banging on about, I've provided a short explanation of the key communities we're featuring throughout the book. If ever you get a little lost and need to check which community I'm referencing, just check back here to remind yourself.

The case study all stars...

- Namrata Sarmah - Women In Product UK

- Danny Hope - UX Brighton
- Vicky Twomey-Lee - PyeLadies Dublin
- Guido Lonetti - Product Tank
- Fiona MacNeill - Ladies That UX Brighton

Namrata Sarmah's Women In Product UK

The first case study we're going to focus on is Namrata Sarmah, who founded and still runs Women in Product UK.

Website: www.wip-uk.com[84]

LinkedIn: https://www.linkedin.com/company/women-in-product-uk[85]

Her community has had exponential growth and supports a wealth of like-minded female product managers and product leaders.

Women in Product UK

So, what is Women in Product UK, I hear you ask.

This strong community offers a free LinkedIn and WhatsApp group as well as in-person and online events sponsored by various brands. Some events are free, and some are paid.

In 2024, an annual subscription was introduced that includes a comprehensive set of offerings, all focused on helping members with their career progression journeys.

The community began in 2020, shortly after Namrata landed her first Chief Product Officer role in the middle of the pandemic.

Although she herself was busy with day-to-day business, the group grew organically through word of mouth before she decided to create a big summer event in 2023 (which had 100% attendance from her invitees!).

The quality of this sponsored event was second to none – and as such, the group's popularity soared. A lot of senior professionals had come along for the journey, which meant the event panels were and still are, often run by CPOs, giving invaluable insight and knowledge (that really cannot be ignored).

The thing that makes this community different is just that. Seniority. Unmatched information and tales of experience. People at the beginning of their careers, therefore, have a wealth of knowledge laid out right in front of them, and as a junior, you wouldn't usually have access to such role models. The member profiles are a differentiator, too. Members come from some of the most inspiring companies in the world, including Big Tech, high-growth startups, global banks, eCommerce, HealthTech, EdTech, Media, Fintech and so on...

A welcome group with an exclusive vibe: Their meet-ups include wines and cheese boards for nibbles, all surrounded by the beautiful interiors of their sponsors' venues.

Namrata's vision is to make it a safe community for members to build peer networks, learn new skills, participate in high-quality events, access experts, coaches, and job opportunities. Plus ultimately – take their careers to the next level. She intends to launch a paid subscription program in May 2024.

So, How Did It All Begin?

Namrata also runs another group called The Career Mums Club.

Facebook group:

https://www.facebook.com/groups/1900723949608737/ [86]

After having her baby in Nov 2017, she saw a gap for bringing together women who are mums but are also career-orientated. It was with this she made a group consisting of executives, lawyers, bankers, doctors, and teachers, who all had one thing in common – being a mum. The group still ticks along today as a Facebook group giving unparalleled support to one another. The group now has 2000+ mums who are all active members, and it's completely free.

In 2020, in the middle of the pandemic, Namrata decided to use her skills of bringing people together to create a community solely for women who work in the dynamic field of product management.

Her team at work wasn't gender-balanced and she felt that as a female leader, she should do something for her people, her tribe.

It began simply as a group on LinkedIn, which spiralled into a lot more.

Before long, the group had reached over 300 members, and the community requested a Facebook group.

Side note – Facebook is great in social media as it allows people to be more open and personal. It's great for growing your community strength without the stiffness of business politeness associated with other platforms.

Off the back of this, a WhatsApp group was made, which now has more than a thousand members. The group acquires circa 100 members per week, and it's all fully organic. Not a penny has been spent in paid acquisition or PR. The followers on social media have been acquired organically too.

Namrata's vast network and the community members amplify the voice that she began, and they, too, bring more members with them.

The community's growth is very much organic but meteoric – and looking at the success of it, personally, I'd put it down to Namrata's dedication. She saw a niche; she filled the gap in the market, and most importantly, she listened to her members.

Her members love the community, and they bring in more members.

As time went on, she went on to create a founding member group of around 30 people who are evangelists of the brand. They help to spread the voice of women in product and strengthen the name and the brand.

They stand on the value of belonging. Belonging to a community where people feel valued, can seek help from experts and can share ideas with like-minded people.

But their strong community is also cherished for its core values - trust, collaboration, kindness, influence, and growth.

Insight from Namrata on How to Gain Paid Subscribers

"The paid subscription is going very well, and our paid events get a lot of sign-ups too.

I'd also like to share that the majority of paid subscribers opt for the higher priced package which is a very interesting user behaviour as typically people go for lower priced packages for subscription products.

My marketing spend is zero, I don't have any sales team either. It's 100% word of mouth and referrals. When acquisition and engagement are solid, retention (hopefully) should be solid too, but we'll know that in a year's time.

I think the secret sauce here is no secret at all, it simply is the value to the customer! People join communities to broaden their network and learn new things, but the ultimate goal for most people is to secure better jobs/opportunities and boost their career growth.

When I designed the paid subscription packages, I always thought of the outcome first, and then worked backwards. Ask the question to yourself - why should I pay for this? What will I get out of this? What is the return on investment (ROI)?

Of course, the events and content quality has to be top notch; the people in the community have to be top notch too. As a Founder, I'm obsessed about the value to the customer. I'd like our members to land bigger & better roles because of Women In Product UK."

Tips from Namrata

• ***Create a community you care about*** - Her first and probably most important tip is to only create a community if you are passionate about it. Don't let others sway you, or do it, as it's the "cool thing to do". To have success, you must always have your heart in it.

• ***Think about what you can give, not take*** - What can YOU give to the community? With building a community, selflessness comes above selfishness. It's not about getting extra sales or getting a leg up in your career. Don't base your event solely around how you're going to get sales or make money from members. Put your heart and soul into delivering something beneficial for them.

So, whether it's offering helpful information or simply providing a support group – make sure your members get something out of it. The community should always come first!

• ***If your offering is good enough, your members will drive growth*** - Namrata's events are of exceptional quality. The entire value proposition of her community is unique and not easy to replicate. The key driver of growth is not marketing but word of mouth and people who had a positive experience with the community.

Danny Hope's UX Brighton

UX Brighton is best known for the lively, stimulating conference it runs for professionals within the realms of UX and other related areas. Each November they meet in Brighton to hear from a hand-picked range of the best speakers on online experience.

Behind the main conference is a thriving community, with other meetups and events, all focussed on sharing knowledge and thinking differently about design, their work and their customers.

About UX Brighton

At the highest level, they aim to raise the quality of design in their specific area. How so? By encouraging people to use human centred design techniques. To make this possible, they give individuals in the community ways of meeting each other and talking together. For people in the industry, they also help to give a leg up on the career ladder – helping members to get into better, more fulfilling jobs.

So, How Did the Community Come About?

Danny had previously tried his hand at event organising and saw how easy it was to pull together. As one of the few UX designers in Brighton at the time, there were few, if any events where fellow industry specialists could chat about user-centred design. So, he did it himself.

> *"I spoke at Brighton BarCamp II and, in the Q&A, mentioned that I was thinking about launching a UX event, then the next day, one of the attendees went and published a website for it, and about 60 people were showing interest."*

The Inaugural Event

The first event was held in the spring of 2008 – and was attended by 60 eager people. The event was split into two parts, the first part a talk. Then the second part was a discussion circle, where everyone introduced themselves and their areas of interest. It had a very big community feel from the very beginning.

In 2011, they were featured in Wired magazine. In the lead up to this there were very few events in the tech industry. And once this began to change the magazine jumped onto the trend and did a full two page spread of all the events around the country. UX Brighton happened to be the third biggest event listed.

The Story So Far...

Commenting on the gradual growth of the organisation and its growth, Danny said:

> *"I was an interaction designer when all this started, and I still am, but I've turned down work for about 18 months. UX Brighton takes up all of my time at the moment."*

Since the first group of 60 eager people, they've grown to their biggest event of over 660. Plus, this year, they're projecting even higher numbers. UX Brighton is an entirely physical event, and they place a lot of value on in-person communities.

How Exactly Did UX Brighton Grow?

In the early days word of mouth was the topmost way that the group grew. There was a lot of demand and not much choice, it was super fertile ground, and it didn't require much legwork. Side note – see the importance of finding your niche!? Everything was free to begin with.

About three or four years ago, the team got more rigorous about it and hired a freelance marketer who was able to stay on top of marketing and sales. At some point, you can't keep doing everything!

> *"We were able to bag a speaker for an evening event who was very high profile. At the time, they*

were one of the most popular TED speakers, and this was back when TED was at its peak. We were so amazed we managed to get this person, and we thought this was a big enough name - we thought we could do a half-day/daylong conference-type event and charge. That speaker pushed us from evening events to conferences that we began to charge for."

Danny's Opinions on In-person Events

"We're humans and humans are adapted for social interactions. You don't get that online. Even if it was super high-resolution video with picture-perfect lighting - it's still not the same. You miss, among other things, the non-verbal communication.

There's a sense of gravity to things that are really happening. You end up having stronger relationships with people.

Serendipity - with online stuff you can only speak to people you've arranged to speak to. In person you're there and you can meet people and build connections that you wouldn't have done online. You can build up rapport."

Tips from Danny on Growing A Community

"It can be stressful. If you're in any doubt, don't bother. You need to be all in, and be prepared to put in the effort.

If you have decided to go for it - see if there's anyone else like you that you can do it as a team. Doing it by yourself is hard. Find people who are interested in the same thing but maybe have different skills e.g. marketing, finance. And ask yourself which bit do I want to do because I'm good at it/enjoy it?

If you can't find someone to come along for the adventure, ask a lot of people for help, and they're almost always willing to help. There's so much willingness out there. But be aware that this dynamic can shift once you start making money. People don't help as freely. And you also can't pester volunteers, if you can afford to pay people, you will need to do that.

We were the first thing of its kind in the world. That's a good place to start. Finding a gap, being ahead of the curve. Be the only people that do that, or the first.

One of the first things I did before we even started was to go out and find people who I thought would have an interest in the group. I did a lot of legwork."

Vicky Twomey-Lee

Mind-blowing growth and extraordinary stories aren't accomplished overnight. It takes time, patience and a sprinkling of magic ingredients. To prove my point, here's another case study of magnificent community evolution. This one focuses on Vicky Twomey-Lee. She's not only a stand-up advocate for the Irish tech scene but also promotes diversity in tech through events, speaking engagements and newsletters.

She is the founder of PyLadies Dublin and the co-founder of both Coding Grace and GameCraft. And, if that wasn't quite enough, she's also a co-organiser of TechFoundHer, organiser of PyLadiesCon, as well as being involved in the Python Software Foundation Grants working group.

She's certainly not a newbie to the big meet-up scene, and if you scan her credentials, you'll definitely want to keep your ears pricked and take some notes from her. Read on to see her top tips!

The Very Beginning

With great success in community-building comes great experience. So, when did Vicky first step onto the scene?

Rewind the clock back to 2004, and she found herself at the very first Python Ireland meetup, nestled comfortably in a pub. With no platforms like Meetup (launched in 2002 but not big in Europe at that time) or Eventbrite on the market yet, the crowd had all met organically (yep – word of mouth is a wonderful thing).

The meet-ups began to grow. Vicky took them under her wing by stepping up to volunteer, and with a need for better resources, they began a shiny new conference. PyCon Ireland started in 2010, chaired by Vicky herself and had over 100 attendees from the very beginning. Side note – PyCon Ireland is still running and growing today!

So, What is Python?

Python is a programming language, a brand-spanking new technology that arrived on the scene in the early nineties. Now, it's used industry-wide and is prolific across the world.

Steve Holden was the Chair of the first PyCon (PyCon US) community conference in 2003. A video on PyVideo titled "The History of Pycon" shows how Pycon (US) came to be.

PyCon slowly grew alongside Python, popping up in new countries across the globe. Vicky credits her time here for gaining expansive knowledge, saying, *"I learned a lot from being there at the right time... and from the leaders in the community as it was so small and close-knit at the time"*.

The Highs & the Lows

Vicky took the role of chair at PyConIE from the very start. Divulging more on that, she admitted it took a lot of commitment, even spending holidays with her husband in Hong Kong sat scurrying away in Starbucks, dealing with programming, sponsors, swag, scheduling, and planning speakers instead of relaxing and unwinding.

It's a really good point to mention because everybody starting out on the journey to breathtaking community numbers should realise that every great feat comes with great commitment.

Nothing comes free in this life – you work hard for it.

But it's not all just hard work. Vicky enjoyed the challenge of chair because it connected her with the grass roots community, sponsors and companies. She was able to begin building relations with speakers and people that would become vital to the growth of PyConIE.

An Advocate for Diversity

Before long, Vicky saw a gap in female attendees to PyConIE. She realised the messaging was wrong and that if they weren't coders, programmers or developers, they felt like they wouldn't fit in.

It was here Vicky became a champion for the minority groups in attendance. She worked tirelessly, asking questions, getting feedback and co-founding several different diversity in tech groups.

She made it her mission to bring people together. To get people interested in tech to try out different areas through running workshops, speaking at events and collaborating with other organisations.

This resulted in multiple diversity in tech events dotted all over Ireland, as well as a newsletter and website to encourage people outside of the tech bubble to enter the community.

Pyladies Dublin

She also founded a group called Pyladies Dublin, intending to give a platform to people who would like to talk at big events but are too nervous to do so. Here, they can speak at smaller, more inclusive group meet-ups and build their confidence. So, they then have the foundations to step up and speak at larger events.

The Importance of In-Person Events

We caught up with Vicky to get her two-pence on the importance of meeting in person.

> *"The whole energy of in-person events is very different than when you're online. No matter how amazing the speaker is, when you're hosting webinars or live-streamed events, people are shy and easily distracted. It's so easy to click 'end' on the steam. Even if people are listening, they can be reluctant to engage. Plus, the incentive to show up live isn't always there because people can just replay the video.*
>
> *With in-person events, the energy is very different. Human nature kicks in, and people naturally come together, start chatting and grab a cuppa. When you are physically at an event, people listen more to the speakers and give the utmost respect.*

At my events, we try to keep our talks short so that people have more time for the rest of the evening, allowing people to create their own break-off groups. You can't have interactions like that remotely. It's a lot more work, but the payoff is immense."

Tips From Vicky

And the moment you've been waiting for, drum roll... some great tips from Vicky.

"Start out with weighing up what you can bring to the table. Ask your contacts if there's anywhere you can use and find a way to cover snacks for the evening. If you can't get somewhere straight off the bat, you can do an initial meet up in a bar, pub or a cafe. Keep it basic and see what's possible in your local area. For example, utilise a cafe that can stay open after closing time if people buy tea, etc. Don't be afraid to ask – the worst they can say is no.

I'd recommend finding a place to advertise your events. A lot of people use meetup or Eventbrite. Meetup is a subscription service, so you'll be out of pocket if you only use it for the first event, whereas Eventbrite charges per event or via subscription, though this is changing too.

See if there is a specific group already around for the meetup you want to do – it may be easier to join suits. Finding linked and similar groups is a great start because you'll find a demographic to spread the word about your meet-up.

With PyLadies I got reimbursements from the Python Software Foundation. PyLadies Dublin is part of a meetup pro network, so we get away with paying the subscription fee, too. So, do a bit of research and check to see if you can get some support. There may be other not-for-profit organisations like Python Software Foundation that help to support local communities with grants and scholarships.

Lastly, don't worry if the numbers are quite small as you're just starting – that's normal."

Guido Lonetti

You've heard about his time at Mind The Product – but as you know, there are two sides to every story. (Or when it comes to the world's most engaged product-focused community, maybe there are thousands of sides to the story!).

So, I caught up with Guido Lonetti. He's a ProductTank organiser for Barcelona and Buenos Aires as well as a Mind The Product coordinator for Latin American meetups.

As you'd probably expect – that comes with a lot of responsibility, organisation skills and all-around event management know-how. So, prick those ears because here's how his story unfolds...

Joining the Mind The Product Movement

Sometime around 2015 in Buenos Aires, Guido and a few colleagues noticed that product craft was growing at a very fast pace. But, contradicting this, there was still no community.

That's where they stepped in.

Discovering Mind The Product and ProductTank, Guido saw the potential for the opportunities of having a broad, world-reaching community that already had meetups happening all over the globe. It set the perfect foundation – because MTP was able to provide them with the right tools to begin organising events from scratch.

Guido delivered his first ProductTank event to 15 switched-on attendees in a humble office. But once word got out, and people started speaking of the meetups, it grew with phenomenal speed and he was soon hosting over 150 people at a time.

One of Guido's personal highlights on the journey was bringing Casey Winters, CPO at Eventbrite and Gibson Biddle, former VP at Netflix to host product strategy talks. He describes having such inspiring speakers as, *"People's product heroes are among the group, and everyone had access to a free masterclass."*

The Community's Growth

Talking about the community's growth – Guido expresses that two of the biggest factors were word of mouth and the calibre of the people that attended.

An infectious spirit meant that the people who first just came to link arms with other product professionals then became ambassadors for ProductTank and began asking to organise their own. That equals growth on growth.

Reflecting on why product people joined to begin with, Guido said, *"the product management career can be very lonely – typically the set-up is one product manager for 6 to 7 engineers, meaning there was a huge desire for peer support, to share best practices and experiences."*

That meant that when people found out about ProductTank it filled a very important gap in the market for a shared product community. One that became a safe space, a place for the sharing of knowledge, a place for product manager therapy!

What Makes a Good Community?

Over the years Guido coordinated more than 20 cities in Latin America, helping them to achieve their goals.

Regarding community success, he reflects, "*the strongest locations I experienced had committed, vibrant organisers. Organisers that would spend the time to make their meetups special. They understand the attendees' interests and send out forms asking what topics the audience would like to hear about. And often, they'll send out satisfaction surveys.*"

It's all about keeping the community members happy.

Consistency is another key thing - some groups would hold three events per year, and others nearly every month. But, keeping things regular ensures your members don't forget about you.

The Power of In-Person

Guido's been around for a long time – he saw the pandemic hit, and he witnessed the impact on community.

At the beginning of the pandemic, there were only digital events – at the time it was great because it meant there were zero barriers around people joining. And they could do so in the comfort of their own home.

In Latin America, everywhere has a similar time zone and so sometimes Guido could achieve an online event with over 20 countries involved and over 1000 attendees. It also meant that there were zero restrictions on who could host. For example, Teresa Torres, a very well-known consultancy speaker, was able to present at one of these events – and it wouldn't have been as simple to get her to come along with an in-person event.

However, as time went on the team noticed a phenomenon – Zoom fatigue.

Attendees would plummet. Why? Their whole life had begun to revolve around a screen. Working from home, chatting with family members from home, now the last thing they really wanted was to log back on to an event in their precious personal time.

People suddenly realised the power of in-person. And now we're back to normality – people, even more so, value networking: the opportunity for laid-back chats and building relationships.

And hey, you can't share a pizza and beer online.

Tips from Guido

Community building is a skill – luckily, one that Guido has perfected the art of.

So, here's some advice from him.

> *"For anybody starting out, my best advice is to team up with other people with different profiles from different companies and different backgrounds. Be a diverse group. Because, while it's not necessarily difficult to lead a community, it's helpful to have*

multiple people working in a coordinated way, looking after their own areas. It gives you time, strength and knowledge.

I've seen communities where there are only two coordinators and the community fails to succeed because the people running them are too busy with their personal work and they don't have enough time on their hands to do it all.

I believe a team of four people is the magic number.

It's also very advantageous for the community itself because they can nurture learning from an array of professionals. At the same time, it's very gratifying for those involved because you get to meet very talented people along the way."

In Summary...

How people's stories unfold differs from community to community, but one thing always seems to remain a constant - and that is how in-person meet-ups hold SO much power.

Another common denominator you'll spot in each of these community case studies is the amount of behind-the-scenes work and dedication it takes to curate and lead a group of people.

I've said it before, and I'll say it again - there's no secret formula to success, but you'll see from the case studies (and my story, too!) that there are some correlations between what works and what doesn't. For example, getting regular feedback, having a strong team network and offering something different from anyone else.

Fiona MacNeill

Fiona is from Ladies That UX Brighton. This international community provides opportunities for those in UX to learn together. The community holds multiple meetup groups in local cities across the globe. A friendly and relaxed environment that is all ears when it comes to everything from problem-solving to peer support.

How It All Began...

Ladies that UX (LTUX) was founded in Manchester in 2013 by Georgie Bottomley and Lizzie Kelly-Dyson. At the time, there weren't a huge number of women in UX, so the group was created as a support network for the small number of people that there were.

Fiona first discovered LTUX Brighton in 2017, being lured to the group by enticing workshops on research methods and design skills. In 2022, Fiona was asked to become the leader of the Brighton chapter thanks to their wealth of knowledge and well-connected familiarity with the UX scene.

Growing the Community

Once Fiona was on board as the new leader, she engaged in several months of intensive networking. Reinvigorating the Brighton chapter through word-of-mouth and rebuilding interest for the group became vital to ensure the growth and support of the community was successful.

The Brighton chapter relaunched in January 2023 and they have gone from strength to strength in growing and building the group.

As a part of the relaunch, they managed to get some inspiring speakers (and great caterers, too!), giving the event an edge that made attendees feel welcome and cherished. This event was for and by them, and this is the template that they follow to this day.

Now in their second year – they've moved solidly into content creation. Their goal? To drum up even more anticipation for each event through solid newsletters and blog content.

Ensuring Success

To make sure the group was gaining traction and loyalty from its members, they held a lot of different event formats. Some of these were quite experimental (e.g. a design walk).

It also proved useful to regularly gather feedback and suggestions from attendees, both via surveys and anecdotally.

The group wants the events to reflect the interests and trends of the local community. Events are always relevant and stretch beyond the expected.

The Value of In-Person

On the importance of creating in-person meetups, Fiona said:

> *"There is no substitute for getting to know people in person. You can only truly get to understand someone's interests and passions this way. There's no online alternative to being able to see the energy in their eyes and the animation in their body when they are engaging in something that fascinates them. Being in the same room with a group of fellow interested people is a uniquely human experience. In a time when so*

much humanity is ebbing away from our day-to-day work, we need in-person meetups to provide a space for connection and embodied collaboration. To know that we are in it together."

Tips from Fiona

Of course, Fiona also carries a wealth of recent community growth experience on her shoulders. So, we had to ask her what her biggest tips are...

"Your strength is in the ideas of other people and always acknowledging and celebrating where those ideas come from. The passion and interest of the people engaged in your community will keep you going during the most trying periods when juggling personal, work, and volunteering commitments can feel overwhelming.

In addition, don't be afraid to ask for help, and this may mean sharing some hard truths. If you are burned out as a leader, nothing can happen, so address this with your group before it happens. If the group has enough momentum, things will continue, and this will allow you to recharge and come back even better!"

HOW TO DEVELOP COMMERCIAL SUSTAINABILITY

"To be considered the best in your industry, you don't need to be the best at any one thing. You need to be good at a variety of complementary and rare skills your industry values and that your competitors lack."

—The Diary of a CEO: The 33 Laws of Business and Life[87]

And so we get to the bit where you try to make some money. Yes, it really is possible. There are many different paths to developing commercial sustainability. You just need to pick the revenue streams that feel best suited to your community. Before you do this, your community needs to be solid. You need to offer something people can't get from your competitors.

But, before you laugh all the way to the bank, let me clear something up first. If your goal is to create a FREE community for people to enjoy, kudos to you, my friend. That's absolutely fine. In fact, many communities flourish for this very reason. They're made by people for people simply because they are passionate about their message.

However, if you want to turn your community into a business that you can eventually sell, well, I have some suggestions for you. Because that's exactly what I did.

If you want to know how to create income streams and how to make money in different ways, this chapter's for you. If you'd rather keep your community free, you can skip to the last chapter.

Where Might Your Audience Have Commercial Value?

This is the very first question you need to ask yourself. Let me give you a real-world example. Imagine you're selling a bike. You need to think about who might find that bike useful .You might come up with things like cycling enthusiasts, people who want to get active, etc.

What's the value proposition of your community? Start by understanding where your audience might have commercial value to others. For example, do they all buy one type of good service regularly? You can even ask them informally in conversation and see what kinds of advertising they all feel they see most.

Is it a niche professional interest group? Recruiting is an expensive business, and a major employer in the town or company within your specialisation may often be willing to support. They get to engage with the community, get the best of the hires, and tell a good PR story about how they support communities, and it's often a lot cheaper than using recruiting agencies!

Agencies might also spend money here to develop their business pipelines for clients and candidates. However, a little word of warning. Be aware of agency reputations and be choosy with your partners! They are a reflection of who you are and the kind of organisations you're happy to support.

Core Income Streams for Communities

If you've got to the point where you want to make money, it's time to consider where you can build some revenue. When it comes to building a community, there are different routes you can go down to start making money. Some examples include:

1. Brand Sponsorships

If you're running a series of online or offline events and you've built up a big enough audience, it shouldn't be too hard to attract the attention of potential sponsors. You're allowing them to reach their target audience where they are active. So, when you first decide what sort of community you want to build, think about what might make it attractive to sponsors.

This is where choosing niche sectors can be smart because then you've got a clear group of potentially interested sponsors. For example, a community for Product Managers may gain more relevant sponsors than say a general business community. It also means the sponsors will be super relevant to your audience, too. It's a win-win.

2. Paid Workshops and Trainings

Another way you can monetise your community is to launch some workshops or put together some valuable training for your members. This can be online or in-person training, depending on what you're able to deliver. Do some research into the core topics your audience wants to learn about and then design some training around this.

If you don't fancy running training courses, then you can look at delivering some sort of online training content that people can access through your community website. For example, a Google Analytics 4 training course for a paid advertising community. Or a copywriting course for writers.

3. Large Paid Conferences

You've read the title of this book. Meetup to Millions. Well, one way that you can attract a bigger audience and grow your community is to set yourself the goal of running large paid conferences.

These conferences can have a lot of reach, and there's a huge potential to expand them into different geographical regions.

If you are able to put on an excellent conference, people will pay a substantial amount in order to be able to attend, particularly if it gives them access to major players in your industry. You can then sell high-priced tickets and aim to attract high-value sponsorship.

Large conferences are an excellent revenue stream for communities. But remember, your small community meetups at the beginning are crucial; these grass roots community meetups were what made Mind The Product so strong.

4. Allow Members to Promote Their Businesses

You've got a large group of people who all care about the same thing. Perfect. They're bound to be able to help each other out. And why shouldn't you encourage them to collaborate? That's what communities are all about. Being stronger together and lending a helping hand where needed. You could create a dedicated area on your website where members are allowed to sell to each other, but they have to pay a fee to have access to this. It may not be a huge revenue stream, but every little bit helps.

5. Industry Insights Reports

Another way you can generate revenue is to regularly produce insightful industry reports based on some of the data you've gathered from your audience and events. You could even team up with one of your sponsors and release a co-branded white paper and charge the sponsor. If you've done your job properly, your audience should completely trust your community, and they're likely to hold any report you produce in high regard.

So, step one here is to find the right major sponsor. Once you've selected your sponsor, they need to agree to sponsor an insight or research report. Then you (the community organiser) publish questionnaires, gather independent data and write up a report. You then get the sponsor to pay to co-brand it, and you're good to go. They can also distribute copies to their commercial audience as well as yours. You should end up with a decent independent report you can put out there. This results in good brand visibility, and it gets shared through your community.

6. Membership Fees

Now, this is a big one. Do you think your online community hub is so valuable that it should be paid for? It's a tough one. You don't want to upset your loyal community. But running a big community also takes a lot of resources and time.

Research shows, paying communities charge $48/mo on average. If you do the maths, you'd earn around $48,000 per month from a community with just 1000 members. So, membership fees are definitely worth considering, but it's not an easy sell and renewals are tough!

If you're delivering consistent value, including training, industry insights and access to important people in your niche, well, people might just be tempted to pay for it. The final decision is yours, but you certainly can charge a membership fee if you feel it's right for your particular community. There's also the option to divide up your community so you have a large section that's completely free, but then people can pay to unlock other parts and gain more value.

7. Digital Products

There are tons of digital products you can create to then offer up to your community, either free or for a reasonable fee. From industry reports (we mentioned this earlier) to detailed ebooks, template documents, apps, webinars, and podcasts, the sky's the limit. Do some research into what your audience will find most useful. Speak to people and find out which digital products would pique their interest.

Video is another option. Got high-quality videos you can use? Then, you could explore putting them behind a paywall. But keep in mind there is a trade-off here. Freely available video is great for growing your audience and community, so they have to choose whether they want to optimise for growth or revenue. There's so much free content out there now. Again, this choice is about whether you want to use videos for growth or revenue.

8. Sponsored Adverts and Content

Not keen on charging your community? No worries. You always have the option of reaching out to relevant businesses and charging them a fee to be able to advertise to your audience. But with this, it's crucial not to bombard your community with irrelevant or annoying ads. You need to be really selective and only work with partners who will be of substantial value to the table.

9. 121 Coaching

Are you a bit of a guru in your field? If you've set up a community, the chances are you know a thing or two! Or perhaps you've got colleagues who are keen to deliver some added value. You can give your community access to 121 paid coaching sessions.

10. How to Maintain Your Income Over Time

The last thing you want is for your community to absolutely smash it, then dramatically crash and burn. So, when you're implementing different revenue tactics, keep the long game in mind. If your community is to stand the test of time, you need to lay down a few strong roots. And by that, I mean solid, trusted partnerships.

Remember, every brand you work with (whether it's early on or in the later stages) is a reflection of what your community stands for. It's never worth teaming up with a company just because of the financial gain alone. Think, what purpose are they going to serve over time? Are they easy to work with? Are they on a similar wavelength?

Poor brand partnerships can be a disaster. They can seem like a match made in heaven, but things can change. Take LEGO and Shell[88], for example. They worked together for around 50 years, and at first, things were great. But when LEGO realised their young audience wouldn't exactly look up to poor environmental practices, they parted ways. Consider how your brands may work together in years to come.

Try to think in broader terms than just a one-off paid sponsorship. If there's a really great recruiter in the space, they might work with you for years. A service, goods or software provider can be a similarly great ally. Consistency and data are key. Show your partners what you're really worth to them, and be consistent enough that they can build plans around you as a strategic partner.

11. Developing a Manifesto to Live By

A manifesto can help you to stay focused on what it is you set out to achieve. This will in turn help maintain commercial sustainability because you're locked in on a goal that everyone agrees on. Publish your manifesto somewhere for all your community to see (and embrace).

A manifesto is "a public declaration of policy and aims." Here's an excerpt from the MTP manifesto[89] to give you an idea of the sort of stuff you can put in there.

> In this discipline you may be an engineer, a designer, a founder or a product manager – all that matters is that you are at the core of the product and passionately work towards the betterment of that product.
>
> This may require fewer people called product managers, but it puts ever more emphasis on the importance of the craft of product management. On learning, sharing and working with others inside and outside our companies in the development of that craft.
>
> This is why Mind the Product and ProductTank exist – to further the craft of product management by bringing together product people of all stripes.

12. Mapping Out All the Different Value Points

What's your audience's attention worth if they make a purchase or get hired? How can your audience bring value to others? But more importantly, how can you bring value to your audience?

13. Understanding Your Place in the Wide Ecosystem

Is your proposition better than anything that's currently out there? Or do you have a bit more work to do to differentiate yourself enough? If your community is strong enough and you can deliver a high-value experience, don't be afraid to charge accordingly.

Benchmarking against others doesn't just mean copying. It means knowing your place in the wider landscape. Everyone spending money has options, so you need to at least be aware of what they're considering.

14. Choosing the Right Partnerships

As I've touched on many times, one of the best things you can do for your community is pick the right partners who align with your values. Don't let the temptation of more money tempt you into working with the wrong companies. Everyone you work with is a reflection of your company and community, so take great care over choosing your partners, suppliers, venues and sponsors.

15. Exploring Different Revenue Streams

You may not be able to pinpoint what will work for your community until you try different revenue streams. Test out what works with your community. If something isn't bringing value or is turning your community off, it's time to reassess.

SPONSOR FEES

Okay, so you're trying to pull in some sponsors. But if you're not a seasoned pro, you may not have the foggiest idea how much to charge. That's OK. I'll explain how to approach setting sponsor fees.

This chapter will help you to figure out how much to charge your sponsors and help you pull together some evidence as to why they should pay a certain amount.

Don't forget, what you're offering will be providing huge value to them. You've practically handed them the perfect audience on a lovely silver platter. Make sure you know what your sponsorship should be worth. Here are some top tips from my personal experience.

When you're trying to successfully pull together a large conference or even a meetup, you're going to need to figure out how to cover costs.

Make Sure You've Got the Bills Covered

Before you set your sponsor fees, you need to consider how much you will need to make to cover the bills. This gives you a number to aim for, and then you can approach sponsors with the goal of achieving a set amount.

A lot of the time, people aim too low. They underprice the value of sponsoring their event and realise that perhaps they could have done better. And you don't want that to be you, do you? So, let's look at exactly how to set your sponsor fees.

The more interesting way to look at it is to determine the value being created or the value of the problem being solved. For example, if you're being sponsored by an organisation looking to generate leads and sales, they will already be generating those leads & sales somewhere else already. So what does that cost them?

You're adding more value too, by bringing them closer to potential customers (which is way more powerful than cheap web advertising) and also offering brand value, by letting them talk in public about how they support communities.

Calculate the ROI for Sponsors

If you know they're going to generate however many leads at your event, you can figure out what each sale is worth to them. This then enables you to talk about what level of return on investment they might see! Which then makes your prices an easy sell. Why would they not pay to be a sponsor if they're seeing such a good ROI?

Every sponsor has a different idea on what a good conversion rate looks like, but the important aspect for the organiser is to at least recognise that ROI does exist and each sponsor will have a view on it. I want to prod them to think about it, not just ignore its existence.

Why Figure Out the ROI for Sponsors?

- It gives you the opportunity to push your pricing a little bit higher and in doing so you create a little bit of a buffer for your community.

- This then allows you to do more for your community, and add some stability and sustainability. It's well worth doing.

In addition, the chances are there's going to be another meet up somewhere or another event somewhere addressing these kinds of people. This could be in the UK, Germany, the US, or somewhere in the world. There will be another place your people gather and sponsors who support it.

That means there's almost always some public benchmarking out there that you can go and take a look at, and again, it's a valuable source of information. It helps to ensure you price in a way that is realistic, so that you will get sponsorship. To put it simply, you must know your market!

Sponsor Packages

When we're thinking about sponsor packages, there's a key element here that we've covered once in this book already. And that's the art of discovery. We talked about this earlier. When looking at your community, what is it they want from you? Do they want to connect with other people? Do they want to learn? What are they looking for?

The same is true for sponsors' responses. Think about Discovery: What is it a sponsor is after from you? Some will be there because they're looking for leads that might lead to new business. Some will be there to recruit new hires. Some will be there because they just want to rehabilitate their brand and show it off to that particular audience!

At which point you could be looking at anything from some logo placement at an event to a promotion offer to your email list. Or you might send a job advert out on behalf of somebody.

Some are looking for things more aligned with positioning themselves, as a thought leader in the space. If this is the case, they might be saying things like, *"perhaps we could do a little talk for you at some point in the future."*

If you do host content, they could provide you with a guest article that you might publish. All of these things can be made up into packages in a variety of different ways. The thing to be careful of here is to remember that what comes first is the community.

So whenever you're considering any ask from the sponsor, check if it's something that your community will appreciate and take value from. If it's just spam and sales pitch, let's be honest, the likelihood is no.

So the responsibility there is on you to guide the sponsor and to say things like, *"We'd love to see a guest article from you, or maybe a short 10-minute speech about a topic. But the responsibility is on you as a sponsor to position yourself as somebody who is bringing something of value to this community. Members come to us looking for educational learning."*

Make sure the sponsor understands: they are not there to do a sales pitch, they are there to provide value, bringing value creation for the audience. So you basically provide the conduit of helping them understand what the audience will really appreciate.

So what's the result you want at the end of their contribution? The main aim is to ensure the sponsor is admired by the audience and not resented. That's where you're looking to get to, but there's a huge amount of freedom there in terms of how that might work!

So it starts with Discovery. You need to ask the right questions. What are the different groups looking for from your community? How can YOU add value and help to identify the common ground where these two groups both win?

Appealing to Recruiters

Finally, on setting your fees - many communities and events in niche communities attract the attention of recruiters - both agency recruiters and in-house recruitment teams. In cases like this, you can look at what the agency might make on a successful placement fee from an intro at your event. In the tech space, for example, this can often be 15-20% on a very significant salary!

Their return on investment will be excellent! From an in-house recruiter perspective, they're looking to SAVE on that agency fee - so they can justify spending money with you. Just be careful to be clear on the behaviours you want to see in your community.

Some parts of the recruitment industry have a name for being a little spammy. They'll usually be happy to play by your rules to be invited back but be sure to consider those rules first and communicate clearly.

Setting Sponsor Fees

Sponsor fees typically very on two key aspects:

- How high value they regard your audience.
- How large your audience is.

If the sponsor is selling high price services, they'll pay more to reach that audience than someone selling something with lower profit attached.

Likewise, a conference with 2000 attendees attracts higher fees than a meetup with 500 people. The range for meetups can be anything from, *"We'll cover the first round of drinks at the bar,"* right up to several thousand pounds contributed to cover everything from drinks to pizzas, and maybe further.

For technology meetups of a few hundred attendees, a sponsor with a high value reason to be there may well be persuaded to contribute in the range of £1000 to £3000.

Smart Payment Terms

Think carefully about when payment should be made, too! Most sponsors like to pay after the event, but they're a large firm, and you're potentially taking costs upfront.

You certainly don't want to see payment terms like 30 days from invoice, so there's often a good argument here for splitting your fee - some in advance, payable immediately, to show their seriousness to hold the opportunity for them. This will help cover any upfront costs you might have and the balance on delivery. Most large firms have processes they'll say are fixed - but in reality, those terms are often negotiable if the right person wants to work with you enough. You're not a bank, so avoid getting into the credit business!

Building Long-Term Relationships

Another mistake people make is thinking about sponsorship as a one event type deal. Nope! You need to approach your sponsors thinking there could be a long-term mutually beneficial relationship on the table, particularly if you plan on scheduling more events.

Don't just sell them advertising at the event. Think about a package you can provide that will bring them additional value. Sponsors love data so create an appealing package that delivers on meaningful data. Ensure that each sponsorship package is tailored to individual sponsors so they feel valued and it doesn't appear as a one size fits all proposition.

And remember, whatever you promise, you need to be able to deliver. So always under promise, over deliver when it comes to the value you deliver your sponsors. Happy sponsors after your first event will be on board for the long-haul and that makes setting up sponsorship for future events a hell of a lot easier!

THE END GAME: HOW TO SELL YOUR COMMUNITY BUSINESS

> *"Online communities have the power for good–to support those in need, to create a shared collective consciousness, and to exchange information and ideas."*
>
> —The Evolution Of Online Communities.[90]

You did it! You're here, at the end game. Well, the point where you'd like to sell your community.

Firstly, hats off to you. You've made it this far. You've built a successful, profitable community. I'm so glad this book has helped you along your journey. But now comes the final bit. And it's perhaps the most important part. You need to convey just how valuable your community is to investors.

I've been there, done that. So, I'd like to share some helpful tips. Let's get started, shall we?

It Doesn't Matter How You Got Here

Communities can take very different routes to get to this stage. Some may have been created from the start with the aim of being sold. Others may have grown from a passion for a particular sector and got so big that selling them just makes sense.

Many people start communities or meetups or other events just for the love of bringing people together and learning from one another. Being able to do this for people feels amazing. You know what else feels good? Seeing all your years of hard work turn into an investment.

There are many examples out there of community-oriented businesses, actually being sold for significant sums of money.

Indeed, in my case with Mind the Product, after a 10 or 12-year Journey and finding our way through the pandemic, we were pretty exhausted by the end of that. The founders were ready to move on and do other things. So, we pursued exactly that route.[91] There are numerous examples on the web of other communities going in similar directions in the past.

Seeing real-world examples of communities that have been successfully bought can be inspiring. For example, inSided was acquired by Gainsight[92], a customer success company. inSided is a customer success community platform that uses communities to increase product adoption and engagement. It helps brands build lasting customer relationships and is used by many companies.

> *"inSided has reimagined communities for the age of Customer Success. By joining forces with Gainsight, we have put ourselves in the best*

position to help companies around the world leverage digital technology to drive all aspects of the customer journey and positively influence NRR at scale."

—Gainsight.com

Selling Strategy

So what's your strategy? If you want to go that route, what options are available to you?

Well, typically, there are two. The first is to sell your event and Community business to a portfolio company, someone who has had other operations like that.

Organisations like Informer or United Business Media own numerous publishing and Conference properties. So they may well consider an acquisition like that.

Now, if you do something like that, you're typically looking at achieving a valuation of something like 6-8 times EBITDA. EBITDA is a profitability measure for accounts. Business broker agents use "multiple" as a rule of thumb for valuing businesses. For example, a conference business valuation, when sold, will often be 6-8 times the EBITDA number. So, six times EBITDA number = business value when sold. For an exhibition business, that multiple might be closer to 8 to 12 times.

Brokers in the space would typically talk about adding your community and event to their existing portfolio. They will then be hoping to generate a little bit more profit from what you do and add that to their bottom line. Or perhaps they'll sell more of their higher-priced events to your audience.

Thinking Outside the Box (or Industry)

Everything I've talked about so far involves pretty much within your industry, but I believe that life gets more interesting if you look at an exit that goes outside your industry.

In the case of Mind the Product and the other example earlier, those exits were actually two vendors in the space - software companies, for example, who need to sell their software constantly.

They look at your organisation and think, this significantly improves our brand positioning. It grants us trusted access to a wide audience of our typical customers. It's essentially a great marketing play for them.

But that means their valuation approach is very, very different. In the case of selling your community operation to a software business, the software that they sell might be thousands to millions a year for a software licence, especially for top-end business software!

Now, when they're selling that sort of product, your audience is worth substantially more to them. And in that case, you can look at very different numbers than if you stayed inside the pure events business.

Having 'That' Conversation

The other thing to consider here is how you might position that conversation and who you might want to turn to. Now, if you've been running for a while, and you've had an array of sponsors along the way, they've already demonstrated that they are willing to spend money in order to work with your community, to reach those people to deliver sales, and improve their brand. There's your first list!

In which case, how do you start that conversation without just going to them and saying, *"Please buy me?"*. If you approach the conversation in that way, perhaps it weakens your hand slightly in the discussions, and you could have done slightly better. You've already shown you wish to get out.

The approach I've used previously and I suspect a number of others have too, is to be a little more cagey than that.

You can go to your existing sponsoring partners and have a conversation that looks a little more like, *"We're looking at the future of our community. Some of the stuff that we want to put more time and resources into. But some of the stuff that we do, we might actually start to wind back a little bit and shrink and we'd really value your opinion as a trusted partner?"*

Now, from there, you can start to assess their response in terms of what aspects they're really interested in seeing you develop. But some of them will often take the bait, and they'll simply ask you the question: *"Hey! Does this mean you're for sale?"*. At that point, you have a much stronger hand.

You're able to say something like, *"We technically don't need to, but I'd certainly be interested in the conversation. What did you have in mind?"*

Get Ready, Set, Negotiate...

At that point, you have a much much stronger negotiating position.

You can potentially drive a better deal, not just for yourself financially but also for the community. You probably care about how they might be looked after from that day forward. Let's be honest: if you've been growing this community for a while, many of these people will be your friends and you'll want to see the whole community well looked after.

Preparing for conversations like this requires plenty of homework! Have you documented your processes and systems so someone else can take them over? Do you have clean, accurate data and permissions?

Be prepared to spend some time elsewhere reading up on this process first, and prepare for it to take some time and involve plenty of lawyers. There are also a number of people who'll help advise you on such a journey.

I continue to work with a few conference and community businesses, but on my first walk through this process, I found Collingwood Associates[93] to be a wonderful team! They run their own events and publishing and offer advisory and coaching services for media, publishing, and event operators. Their content is excellent!

Always Visualize Your Desired Outcome

Most of all, on this part of the journey, spend some real time reflecting first on what kind of outcome you want? Is the driver for you purely financial? Or are you looking to find an acquirer that shares similar values? Do you want someone who is willing to invest in the community for the long term?

The End Game is a Big, Emotional Deal

Be prepared for the emotional journey - this has no doubt consumed much of your attention for some time. It will feel like a major thing when you do finally get to closing the deal. You're letting go of something you've poured your heart and soul into (and sometimes, blood, sweat and tears!).

With Mind the Product, that journey was over a decade in the making! So many members of the community became firm friends and indeed still are. The people on our team had indeed become family.

Companies often say that, but with Mind the Product, we ran international conferences from 2015 through to 2023. We flew together, stayed in hotels, and had fun excursion days! Over this journey we'd all become hugely emotionally invested both in the community and in each other.

That doesn't mean it was an easy exercise though, recognizing that we'd be putting all these efforts and dear friends in the long term care of others. Part of the sale process for us was about trying to find a home that had the financial resources to support continued investment and growth in the community. Plus, a home where there were some deep shared values.

Should You Put Together an Investor Deck?

I actually wouldn't recommend it. Investors in startups have a fairly stable approach of what they're looking to see, so decks in this space can be formulaic.

When you're selling a community, event and media business, it's a very different situation. The nature of the potential buyers will be widely different. For example, ranging from another event business to a software business in the case of Mind the Product.

This means they'll have very different outcomes in mind and will all want to see very different information. Spend time ensuring your data and your finances are clean and tidy. You'll also want to make sure any systems and processes are well documented.

From there, it's going to be a more fragmented approach as you learn what each potential buyer holds dear! They will focus on different aspects depending on their specific interests, so you're unlikely to find one size fits all.

You may find a one page overview useful at the start of the conversation, but not much more! This might cover the size and demographics of the attendees and community members, the headlines on last year's financials, a summary of events, and what you see as the key value proposition to potential acquirers.

Beyond that, they will all be asking unique questions anyway. Some will dig into the audience and reach, some into finances, others might be more interested in content libraries or any trademarks you hold. It's your job to deliver the goods and provide them with everything they need to make an informed decision.

6 Top Tips for Selling Your Community

1. Keeping Interested Parties Interested

Send regular updates to people who might be interested in buying. Keep them in the loop, always. If they see your community is doing amazing things, they'll start to become a warm lead. Sign them up for your newsletter, and follow them on social platforms. Send them personal email updates. Do whatever you need to do.

2. Keep Developing Your Revenue Streams

Investors are looking for a business that's already successful, and an audience who are engaged. You'll need a lovely platter of revenue streams to pitch to investors. So, continue to improve your revenue streams, or be able to show ideas of where future revenue growth might be found.

3. It's All About the Warm Pitches

Right from the start of your journey, work hard to build strong working relationships with people inside and outside of your community. Become a thought leader. Put in the effort to catch up with people in person. You never know when this will pay off. Cold selling is extremely tough. You want your prospects to be warmed up, toasty, in fact! And if they can be persuaded by someone else who is singing your praises, that makes your job a hell of a lot easier. Make connections with people who will champion you and your community.

4. Know Your Worth

Look, you've built something you're really proud of. It's your community. It should not be undervalued. So be wary of what offers get thrown your way, and make sure you've got stellar legal advice. And if an offer sounds too good to be true, don't pass it up, but be wary and have your guard up. Don't be tempted to sell your community for anything less than you think it's worth.

5. Check Out the Competition

Look, if you want to persuade an investor your community is worth it,[94] you need to know what you're up against. So, do some decent competitor research. You need to be able to differentiate yourself. Why is your community better, stronger, more unique?

6. Gather Data

Make sure you've got a whole bunch of data to support your cause. Pull together testimonials, case studies and revenue info that you can use to put into your investor deck. They're going to need some decent numbers to make them look twice. Dig around and find the most powerful stats and results. These numbers could make or break your sale.

Congrats on getting this far, but be aware, selling your beloved community will be emotional.

Make sure you've got all your ducks (or data) in a row. Do all the groundwork so that if an investor asks for some info, you've got it to hand.

Be clear on your outcome. You don't want to get to the sale stage and dive head first into negotiating if you don't know what the end game is. What does success look like?

Put together a clear selling strategy, think outside the box, research competitors and be prepared to negotiate!

Think long and hard about what you'd like your involvement to be after the deal is signed. Most acquirers will want some of the original team to stick around, but is that really what you want? Make sure to consider all the options, and take good legal advice on any clauses that surround these aspects.

GROWTH: HOW TO TAKE YOUR COMMUNITY FROM 20 PEOPLE TO 300,000

Alone vs. Together

> *"Alone we can do so little, together we can do so much."*

> \- Helen Keller, 1980. (Helen and Teacher: The Story of Helen Keller and Anne Sullivan Macy)[50]

It's certainly true that individuals can achieve incredible feats. You can't deny that. But the power of a group of people who share a passion for something is almost limitless.

I'm not disputing that when you're alone, you can have lightbulb moments, big ideas, and make an impact.

But together? Together we can spark the electricity to make that lightbulb shine. Together we combine our expertise. Together we combine our knowledge and our strengths – together, we're unstoppable.

After all, it's human nature

Have you got that yearning to grow something really special? I get it.

In fact, it's human nature to want to be part of something bigger.[51] If we join or create a group, it satisfies our deep, burning desire to belong. In fact, most of the things we humans have achieved have been done in groups. Building the pyramids? Groups. Travelling to the moon? Yep, done in a group. Creating crucial vaccines? That'll be groups too.

> *"When group members learn to work together as a cohesive team their success becomes more certain."*
>
> —Donelson R. Forsyth, University of Richmond, 2019. (The Psychology of Groups)[52]

Those who know me well will know that Mind the Product has been both my work and my passion for over a decade. It's an events and media business built on a core foundation of community and belonging.

Groups of people around the world meeting up regularly for professional learning and support. One of my earliest memories of working with that organisation was a first time attendee telling me she found the experience to be fundamentally: professional therapy! That's when I felt we'd created an important communication channel for these professionals, and it was having a profound effect on people individually – feeling that sense of belonging. Being seen and heard by others is important to all of us. It's a crucial part of belonging.

Everyone, at their core, wants to belong. So all you have to do is create a community people want to belong to. Give them a cause and tap into this need.

We are ingrained to want to learn, to engage and connect with others who share our values.

From the ripe old age of four,[53] we begin to want to be part of a group. Children start to enjoy joining sports teams and start to cooperate more with others. This deep-rooted human behaviour stays with us throughout our life.

Here's a little insight into the social development of a four year old.

> *"There is an increased awareness of other people's minds, which allows children to develop negotiation skills, resolve conflicts verbally, monitor the emotional state of a group, and regulate other children's behavior."*
>
> –What Toddler Social Development Looks Like[54]

We have an in-built desire to form a bond with others, and that's the fundamental reason that we believe building a community really is the secret to success.

It Starts with You

Building a community starts with you. The future of your community is in your hands. This book will help you put your dreams into action.

I've had the pleasure of working with a brand that went from just 20-something product people to over 300,000 dedicated members of a strong community. So I guess it's only right to compile all my tips and tricks to help you do the same. All I can ask in return is that you keep helping others as you go on a Journey. Karma comes back around.

Luckily, I've gone over the hurdles and backed out of the dead ends, so I can open your eyes to the right way to grow your community (with a lot less U-turns or fumbling through the dark necessary).

How Does a Community Grow from Nothing?

So – how do you grow a community? It's not just setting up a group chat, an online forum or an email hitlist (although this is definitely a part of it too!) – instead, it starts with passion.[55]

Back in 2010, when the inaugural ProductTank meet up first took place in the back room of the Ruby Blue pub, it was our shared passions that brought us all together; where the flame was first ignited.

It didn't take long for the ball to start rolling, and before long, we welcomed more and more members to our growing community.

As those early meetups grew quickly by word of mouth, we often found them over subscribed! We were getting to the point where hundreds of people would RSVP the moment the announcement went out, so we had to really carefully control numbers and also issue reminders — *"If you can no longer make it, please cancel your RSVP so someone else can attend"*. The technology available for this all has terrible user experience (UX) — meaning RSVP's don't get updated and attendee numbers are out of sync with organiser expectations (and even catering or safety limits!).

Namrata's community, Women in Product UK, is an excellent example of a community growing through word of mouth. She set up a free LinkedIn and Whatsapp group, and these micro communities grew from there. However, this doesn't mean you can just create a LinkedIn group, sit back and watch members magically appear. The timing has to be right and you need to have the right people in the group who are happy to champion your cause. The next step to growing a community from nothing is to hold a successful event. This can often be the key turning point for many communities. A make or break moment.

That first event can go very, very well, or it can completely tank. You need to deliver real value to the people who choose to give up their time to be there. And if they feel they've gained a lot from the experience, they'll not only attend again, but they'll be happy to shout about it.

Part of the reason why Women in Product UK was such a success was simply down to their first event. In her own words, *"the quality of this sponsored event was second to none."* Their meet-ups include wines and cheese boards for nibbles, all surrounded by the beautiful interiors of their sponsors' venues. Plus, people got access to senior women in product with a wealth of experience to share, and there was no other place where people entering the industry could get this.

She went the extra mile to ensure this event was a hit. People had an extremely positive experience and the group took off from there.

Fiona MacNeill from Ladies that UX Brighton put on a memorable first event that significantly contributed to the community's success going forward.

"We managed to get some inspiring speakers (and great caterers, too!), giving the event an edge that made attendees feel welcome and cherished. This event was for and by them, and this is the template that they follow to this day."

—Fiona MacNeill, Ladies That UX Brighton

Danny Hope's UX Brighton experienced rapid growth thanks to a successful first event. It was held in the spring of 2008 – and was attended by 60 eager people. The event was split into two parts, the first part a talk. Then the second part was a discussion circle, where everyone introduced themselves and their areas of interest. It had a very big community feel from the very beginning. All the successful community owners I've spoken to were able to foster a real sense of community right from that very first event.

"Start out with weighing up what you can bring to the table. Ask your contacts if there's anywhere you can use and find a way to cover snacks for the evening. If you can't get somewhere straight off the bat, you can do an initial meet up in a bar, pub or a cafe. Keep it basic and see what's possible in your local area. For example, utilise a cafe that can stay open after closing time if people buy tea, etcetera. Don't be afraid to ask – the worst they can say is no."

—Vicky Twomey-Lee

Let's circle back to Mind The Product. We were working on securing events and creating an environment where people could share knowledge and network.

At one point, we were sizable enough that we could have regular cash sponsors for a couple thousand pounds each event. This allows us to rent the local school hall for those evenings and bring in a couple of bar staff and drinks. Using a school hall was a good way to give some funds back to the local community, but it also meant the AV would often be in disarray when we arrived. Turns out, school kids can have real fun with speakers, microphones and projectors, so we never know what configuration we'd find when we arrived.

An in-person environment was how we grew our community: a place where others on the same page could all meet one another, contributing ideas, experience, and expertise.

And I believe that's all it takes to start growing your community, too. A shared passion, a mind to pick, a setting where people feel welcomed (and although our setting was in-person, this could be within the online world for you).

So, how do you take that first leap of faith, and who do you take with you on your journey to making your vision a reality?

Define Your Audience

Identify your audience – ask yourself: Why is your community different from any others?

This will help you to figure out the members you'd like to attract and how you'll ultimately go on to grow.

If you've already got a team of like-minded individuals or even just a few trusted alliances, then great! It's probably the right time for you to test the waters by bringing these people together.

This could be via an online platform, social media,[56] or, like we did – at a physical location.

Always consider the important things: it should be accessible for your target group and support the interactions you intend to take place. For example, if you want to initiate the group with a speech, then ensure your platform can do that (i.e. don't let the Zoom free trial cut out on your speaker after 40 minutes - it's just awkward!).

It doesn't have to be anything grand or glamorous. In fact, when our very first community meetup took place, the dark alleyway that led us into that pub room was a stark contrast to the passion that enlivened our spirits, desires and communication.

But what if you don't already have a team? As you'd probably guess, it's easier to get an initial outreach when a few of you are already on the same page. But actually, many powerful communities we've had the pleasure of seeing grow have started with just one solo person. If you have passion – check? And commitment – check? Then it only takes YOU to begin the traction.

Plant the Seed; Grow the Tree

As you begin the journey of creating online and offline events,[57] you will become aware of your weaknesses, the gaps you'd love another to help you out in. After all, none of us are perfect! Always ask people what they want - and then ask for help if you want this to thrive. I wasn't afraid of bringing in people to do things who I knew would do a better job than me.

Danny Hope from UX Brighton has a few very wise words to share on the importance of asking for help!

> *"If you have decided to go for it - see if there's anyone else like you that you can do it as a team. Doing it by yourself is hard. Find people who are interested in the same thing but maybe have different skills e.g. marketing, finance. And ask yourself which bit do I want to do because I'm good at it/enjoy it? If you can't find someone to come along for the adventure, ask a lot of people for help, and they're almost always willing to help. There's so much willingness out there. But be aware that this dynamic can shift once you start making money. People don't help as freely. And you also can't pester volunteers, if you can afford to pay people, you will need to do that."*
>
> —Danny Hope, UX Brighton

Guido Lonetti from the Mind The Product Team also has some wisdom to share here.

> *"For anybody starting out, my best advice is to team up with other people with different profiles from different companies and different backgrounds. Be a diverse group. Because, while it's not necessarily difficult to lead a community, it's helpful to have multiple people working in a coordinated way, looking after their own areas. It gives you time, strength and knowledge.I've seen communities where there are only two coordinators and the community fails to succeed because the people running them are too busy with their personal work and they don't have enough time on their hands to do it all."*
>
> —Guido Lonetti

By the time we got to the first conference, we had a small army of people who wanted to volunteer and help out. One of them was actually so effective on the day, we ended up offering her a full time job with the team helping with events. She was so effective in ways others on the team were not that we eventually asked her to stop right up - offering her a board seat as our Chief Operating Officer. Analisa was a lynchpin for so many achievements on that journey.

And it won't be long before you'll find people within the community that you want to bring along on the ride. MTP did this from the early days. We found people who were happy to champion our cause, including some who were at the very first meetup.

Namrata's Women In Product community harnessed the power of community champions. A founding member group of around 30 people was created. These people were evangelists of the brand. They help to spread the voice of women in product and strengthen the name and the brand.

Danny Hope of UX Brighton says:

> *"Ask a lot of people for help, and they're almost always willing to help. There's so much willingness out there. But be aware that this dynamic can shift once you start making money."*

So, my advice to you is: Put your plans out there – plant the seed, arrange the meetup. Let your metaphorical tree's branches go absolutely wild, because before you know it, you'll organically have others on your team.

We actually hired two people from the conference volunteer crew to join the team as full time employees. They understood what we were about, understood the audience, and each of them came with skills that we needed to continue growth. Over the period that followed, a number of other hires came via people known to us in the community. Multiple nationalities were represented as we grew and some very different backgrounds, but all with a core love of what we stood for - building a community where people could come together in psychological safety, learn and grow.

After the first conference afterparty (2012), the venue had hit a minimum spend at the bar. We didn't quite hit that, so as they closed down they snuck one of our crew out of the back door with a couple cases of champagne to make up the numbers. They went back to his house that evening, and were never seen again!

We really did put community at the heart of everything we did for MTP. For every annual conference, at least one of the speakers on the main stage would be someone who's never done a major conference before. We'd heard them speak at a smaller meetup, loved what they'd had to share, and offered to coach them on how they might bring that to a wider audience. Raising voices was a key part of our curation effort.

UX Brighton also recognised the importance of selecting the right speakers. For them, one big name speaker helped them tap into the conference market.

> *"We were able to bag a speaker for an evening event who was very high profile, at the time, they were one of the most popular TED speakers, and this was back when TED was at its peak. We were so amazed we managed to get this person, and we thought this was a big enough name - we thought we could do a half-day/daylong*

> *conference-type event and charge. That speaker pushed us from evening events to conferences that we began to charge for."*
>
> —Danny Hope, UX Brighton

Guido Lonetti, ProductTank organiser for Barcelona and Buenos Aires as well as a Mind The Product coordinator for Latin American meetups reflected on nailing speakers when I spoke to him. He said one his personal highlights on the journey was bringing Casey Winters, CEO at Eventbrite and Gibson Biddle, former VP at Netflix to host product strategy talks. He describes having such inspiring speakers as *"People's product heroes are among the group, and everyone had access to a free masterclass."*

Later in your journey, once you've established a more stable group of members, you might also want to pick ambassadors and moderators. They can help to keep the community in check and guide new members along the way, but for now, let's keep it low-key...

You want your first meet up to be a success, but how do you make that happen? Define your community's purpose and give your attendees a reason to join. (We all need a kick of motivation sometimes, right?).

Passions Unite

Make sure your group of attendees has an appetite for the topic. You'll also want to check everyone is aligned with the desired outcome of the meetup with an agreed expectation of what it entails.

So, whether you're a group looking for networking opportunities, an assembly of eager-to-learn individuals yearning to expand, or you're all after a fiery debate – make sure everyone is on the same page. Because ultimately, that's what will fuse the very first connections and communications in your community.

For Women In Product UK, the audience was key. It was ultimately what helped to grow such a powerful community. A lot of newbies in the early stages of their careers were absolutely thrilled to be able to meet and chat to more senior members in the industry. This created such a valuable proposition. Juniors could pick the brains of some of their role models and listen to expert panels share their inside knowledge. The community had an impressive array of member profiles from some of the most inspiring companies in the world including Big Tech, high-growth startups, global banks, eCommerce, HealthTech, EdTech, Media, Fintech and so on.

Namrata's vision was to make it a safe community for members to build peer networks, learn new skills, participate in high-quality events, access experts, coaches, and job opportunities, plus ultimately – take their careers to the next level.

All Aboard

Next up, onboarding. When it came to Mind The Product, most people initially found the meetups - or should we say stumbled across the meetups - in a bid to discover the answers to all of their burning questions.

The onboarding process wasn't entirely polished in the earlier days. But being able to help others solve their everyday dilemmas and to provide them with a place to connect with peers made the group instantly feel like a part of something special, the kind of place people wanted to be involved with.

Don't worry too much about fine-tuning this kind of detail so early on. It's something that will advance as the community grows.

Community Identity

Your community's identity[58] is essential for its success. Your members need to feel like they belong[59] and have influence – it's why I'd recommend starting small and gradually building your group.

This ensures the passion grows authentically and that you instil the right excitement in each person from day one. It also encourages people to participate, to stand up and talk above the chatter (because hey, unless you're the world's most confident person, it's natural to get the jitters when speaking in front of big crowds that you haven't gotten to know yet - don't kid yourself). There's always room for improvement with a little practice.

Interaction and communication are key at your first event (and, well, every meetup for that matter). It's so important to always look for meaningful ways to spark conversation, because the more each member talks and debates, the more they unravel themselves, the more you can understand their desires and the more people will find a connection to them. This gradually sparks the same flame in more and more minds.

Heard of social comparison theory? In 1954, a psychologist called Leon Festinger[60] developed this concept. He believed that people want to unite with others to reflect on whether their own beliefs are accurate. People seek to compare themselves with others who are a similar age or occupation. Perhaps this is why these niche communities work so well because people in the group have similar interests and career aspirations.

The communities that really take off organically tend to be ones where there's a real need. If there's nothing like your community out there and demand, you're all set. Take UX Brighton for example. Danny Hope was one of the few UX designers in Brighton at the time. There were few, if any events where fellow industry specialists could chat about user-centred design. So, he did it himself.

> *"I spoke at Brighton BarCamp II and, in the Q&A, mentioned that I was thinking about launching a UX event, then the next day, one of the attendees went and published a website for it, and about 60 people were showing interest."*

-Danny Hope, UX Brighton

Are you filling a gap in the community world? Having a clear community identity and purpose from the getgo will serve you well.

Keep on Growing; You've Done the Hard Part

So, you've held your first event with a small engaged group, now what?

Use this as your learning curve. This is your first of hopefully many meetups, and everyone has room for improvement – trust us.

By engaging with and listening to your members' feedback, you can find out what they want more of, what they want less of, what worked and what didn't and what they really, truly want from a community.

This knowledge will help you to tailor the itinerary of your next meet, and increase satisfaction. Happy members = loyal members.[61] And loyal members are more likely to recommend, invite and endorse your community to others – the sort of stuff we love.

This isn't just integral after your first event but every event you hold. As your community grows, it's important not to get arrogant – there's always room to learn and expand, no matter how big you end up growing.

Putting Your Name in Their Mouth

That leads us to an essential ingredient to throw in the mix, which is required to achieve steady growth – word of mouth.[62] The great news is as your community gets bigger, each and every single new member will have another branch of other like-minded folks they know. It could be anyone, from inspired and eager-to-learn colleagues to social buddies ready to be recruited into the bigger picture.

With Women in Product UK, after starting a LinkedIn group initially (and growing to around 300 members) the community requested a Facebook group. Facebook groups are quite different to LinkedIn or Whatsapp, for some reason people seem to be more open and personal. It's great for growing your community strength without the stiffness of business politeness associated with other platforms.

Off the back of this, a WhatsApp group was made, which now has more than a thousand members. The group acquires circa 100 members per week, and it's all fully organic. Not a penny has been spent in paid acquisition or PR. The followers on social media have been acquired organically too.

Her members love the community, and they bring in more members. Word of mouth is so powerful.

The great thing about word of mouth? A lot of word of mouth is organic. When they love something they'll tell others.[63] I'm sure you, yourself, have spent a Monday morning at the office gathered at a work friend's desk, telling them all about a must-have place, event or news article, right?

But word of mouth doesn't have to be purely organic – you can encourage it, too. This can look like sharing online or even approaching members of the community and asking them who they'd recommend joining the troop or who they think could add value to the conversation. Why not consider incentivising engagement too?

People unite over a common cause. If you can unite people over a common mission (to help women in product advance their careers or grow a community for product managers to thrive), then your community will spread like wildfire. Humans yearn for something in common. We unite in groups when we feel we're working towards something important.

Why are psychologists so fascinated with group behaviour? [64] Because most of what we do as humans is in groups (learning, playing, working and even sleeping). Your goal is to make your group so united in their shared interest, that they feel compelled to spread the word.

Always Add Value

Of course, once you get a new member through the door, whether it's through word of mouth or simply through your expanded growth, the next step is retaining them.[65]

Retaining their knowledge, their participation, and their spot in your community.

How? It's simple. It's by adding **value** to their time.

> *"A man who dares to waste one hour of time has not discovered the value of life."*
>
> —Charles Darwin

Time is precious – we all know that, in fact, we all wish for more of it (apart from at 4.55 pm on a Friday afternoon, when the pub is calling your name). So, why should someone use their time to be a part of your community?

What value are you adding to their life? That value could be knowledge, peer support or networking insight – but whatever form that value comes in, it needs to be clear before they invest their time in you.

Let's rewind a little; I mentioned that value could be several things. But in my experience, the most powerful values and motivators to bring people to a meetup are:

- Knowledge – the chance to learn, to mentally develop, to improve a skill set.[66] This can accelerate a career, leading to promotions and pay rises. Now you're not only having fun, you're being rewarded.
- Togetherness – having a support system, a shoulder to lean on, an ear to chew.
- Networking – a chance to meet professionals and stay up-to-date with the latest industry developments.

Of course, there are other components, too, like resources, tools and awards (ahem, don't forget the free beer!). We started the London events with sponsors covering the cost of beer, but remember to tailor to the local culture. The first meetup we ran in California had people walking through the door and ignoring the beers - they wanted Kale smoothies!

You might be wondering how we found initial sponsors within such a small group. Well, we kept a close eye on those applying to join the group. If we saw applications from people with titles like "Sales Manager" or "Recruiter" we would turn them down but tap them for sponsorship:

"The group is only for active Product Managers and we keep membership tight to maintain the quality of the conversations. If you'd like to access this group for commercial reasons, we do welcome such partnerships, and sponsorship details are available."

Stand Out from the Crowd

What makes your events, and ultimately your community, different from others? As with everything in life, you've probably got competitors in the field – what do these competitor communities lack? There's almost always a gap, and it's your job to find out what it is and fill it. Ask! Don't Guess. Guessing is based on personal bias. Asking is data driven. Ask key industry figures. Get them to fill out a survey. Gather data on what people feel they are missing. Set up a Slack group with people who are passionate about your topic and ask them questions.

Once you've established a meetup for your community that works and have set a regular structure for your events, it's time to expand your outreach. But how, other than just word of mouth?

Be Here, Be There, Be Everywhere

Use different platforms – be visible and at hand at every touch point. This could be in-person meetups, online webinars, social media groups[67] or even a regular newsletter. Fiona MacNeill from Ladies that UX Brighton has said that she plans to create engaging content to boost awareness of their events. The plan this year is to drum up even more anticipation for each event through solid newsletters and blog content.

It only takes a small Google search to discover a whole world of networking opportunities among the obvious big players. I've seen communities grow on all kinds of platforms before. Maybe the most important thing to be sure of is that the member experience is enriching, and you can get valuable insight from it too.

Our plan of attack, with Mind The Product, was being consistently present across all of the major social platforms at that time - LinkedIn, Twitter, Facebook. Think about where your people are likely to be - maybe it's TikTok! Concurrently, our very carefully curated weekly newsletter dropped into the mailboxes of our loyal members – packed with enough information to engage but short and snappy enough not to waste their time. No one wants waffles, that's for sure.

We also networked to our heart's content – attending and supporting similar events and communities. By putting ourselves out there, we were completely visible across the whole tech world, meaning there were absolutely no missed opportunities to meet like-minded individuals. When our team members went to other unrelated tech events for example, we'd often put a message out to any like-minded souls we met. We'd give them a time and location and tell them to bring others who might be interested in such a meetup, gradually word spread, and a new location joined our network.

The Online Multiverse, The Place to Be Seen

So, moving on – you've become an expert at in-person events, but without the personal touch of meeting together, how do you make the online side of your community stand out from the rest? In our eyes its content, content and more content.

In the same way that your in-person group wants added value – your online community does too. Give them a reason to get involved at every touchpoint. Why not give them a sneak preview of the upcoming agendas to spark extra excitement and interest, or have exclusive guest speakers that can add an extra string to your bow.

Plus – as with anything, be trustworthy. Don't over-promise. Secure your credibility with a reliable experience that seamlessly transitions through every single platform you use.

When you have trust, it will empower your members to have enough confidence to interact with other members in meaningful ways.[68] It may seem obvious, but when trust is present, the people in your community will feel included – like they're at home.

The community you've built isn't just a group of people sharing the same common interests; it's a web of relationships. It's your job to ensure these relationships are nurtured – through personal conversations, group learning and interactive events. With value, trust and nurturing, your community will have a sense of belonging and strengthen the entire group of members.[69]

This doesn't get talked about much, but it's hugely important. You also need to be aware of the safety of your attendees. Not just their physical safety, but also psychological. Setting rules and boundaries and a clear code of conduct can help avoid any awkward or potentially damaging situations for people. You need to ensure people feel safe sharing their ideas and if there are any debates, that these are handled in a respectful way.

Over to You / What Are You Waiting For?

I hope this handy 101 guide, along with the story of how we grew our community, has fuelled you with the passion, tools and inspiration to go out there and grow your own community.

Bear in mind – growing a community is an ongoing process. Nothing authentic multiplies overnight, and it takes hard work, strategy and commitment to attract members. But, with patience, dedication, and most importantly, that underlying flame of passion – you too can build a community from scratch. Plus, you'll also benefit from HUGE personal and professional growth. What's not to love?

IN CONCLUSION...

You made it to the end! Yep – this is where we scribble down the last few words and move on to publishing. We know that a number of you have been waiting on this book for a while!

So, thank you. Thank you for waiting and thank you for reading. I think it's always good to end on a high, right? So to round up the book, I'd like to touch on some of the things I'm most proud of. It's always tempting to stay humble and avoid shouting about our achievements, but I'm going to give it a go.

The Bits I'm Proud Of

Everyone has achievements they want to shout home about – here are a few of mine.

No greatest feat list of mine would be without swirling into the accomplishments of Mind The Product. My time here taught me the power of community and events: the true value of togetherness. I fell in love with this industry almost straight away, and I'd be more than honoured to work within it for time to come. As long as it'll let me!

Mind The Product really did put Product Management on the map as a discipline. It was already happening across the pond in Silicon Valley, but Mind The Product took the reins, steering it globally and accelerated its growth. Product managers across the world were finally being provided with a fresh-faced community, one of which delivered one-of-a-kind content, learning resources and peer support. It was new and refreshing.

It's easy to sit back and ignore the bigger picture sometimes – but the brand actually managed to ask the harder questions and get people involved. Tech can sometimes get a bit excited and run away with itself – building products *"just because we can"*.

In the famous Marc Andreessen quote, he alleged, *"software is eating the world"*. [95] I would argue that if he's right, it's Product Managers who are writing the menu.

Mind The Product actually challenged what people put out there. Martin Eriksson, Emily Tate and Marc Abraham would put product people and business leaders on stage to ask them the harder ethical questions[96] and challenge the assumptions. The voice of reason, some would say. Our curation was regarded as some of the very best in the tech world.

One of the things of which I'm most proud of is that Mind the Product was able to give stage time to so many voices across the world, those who asked technologists to think just a little more deeply.

Throughout my time at Mind The Product – from the first initial meet-ups to the huge around-the-world conferences one thing remained a constant. That this community provided a safe space and a home to so many like-minded individuals. In a world where it's easy to feel alone – you really can't get better than feeling like you're a part of something.

Personally and in terms of career impact, the thing I often really enjoy, and I think is actually something of a superpower when it comes to start-ups, is that not only can I find great people to work with (once a recruiter – always a recruiter!) but I can then often get them incredibly enthused about the direction of travel.

Aside from my own startup adventures, I've been lucky enough to be invited to advise a number of others along the way. Being able to mentor and support others in a personal capacity brings me so much joy, and I'm proud to witness first hand the value that I can add to others lives, careers and communities.

But actually, it really helps towards my own development to be constantly exposed to different problems, customers and mindsets! It's like a challenge in itself – with the reward coming from every angle.

We've covered so many different aspects of the Mind the Product journey here, but as with all Products - it's time to launch this one so we can get some real feedback. We'd love to hear from our readers on what you feel we could go deeper on. If the demand is there, a second edition OR a follow up book may well become a thing!

As I covered in the Preface, I've been hit with some extremely challenging health issues which have led to us really wanting to get something out there. We've pulled the latter bits of this book together in between procedures, treatment and recovery - which has been no small task! However, despite everything, we're really proud of the story we've put across and the amount of genuinely actionable and useful advice this book contains.

I'd love to chat with you about any elements of the book. Please do feel free to search me out on LinkedIn and drop me a note. I'm all ears! If there's anything that you'd like to see covered here that we've not addressed, or rather, please do tell us which aspects have been the most helpful to you! As any community does, we thrive on feedback. If you've found this book enjoyable and helpful, show us some love and support in the reviews and online.

Stay tuned, and we'll be back with round two before you know it.

Thank you.

AFTERWORD

Finally, we'd like to hand over to Todd Olson[97] for the closing words. Todd is the Founder and CEO of Pendo[98]. They're a world leading software company who have the world of meetups very much in their origin story too. They are the business who ultimately acquired Mind the Product, so over to Todd:

Why would a software company care about community and meetups? It's a good question - it's hard to imagine people looking to buy software at a community meetup. In fact, meetups are part of Pendo's founding story and a core strategy that's led to its success.

Back in 2014 before Pendo had raised significant capital, acquired many customers, or even had more than a dozen team members, we were trying to grow awareness amid a sea of fellow tech companies. It was incredibly hard to do it online — how do we compete with companies vying for the top spot on Google Adwords on a limited budget? And we were operating in the nascent market of product tech that frankly, needed to build awareness for itself. ProductCamps were local volunteer-run meetups held on weekends, much like the ProductTanks that James and team created. Product people would pitch their ideas for talks, and the top vote getters would deliver those talks in an impromptu conference format over the course of the day. Companies would sponsor these events for a very reasonable fee, and set up a table and hand out swag. Pendo started attending these meetups very early in our company's history. We'd capture interest through a simple paper sign-up sheet, and we'd often host a thought leadership session. Our early customers were predominantly located in the cities where we attended these events: Atlanta, Austin, Toronto, Boston, and more.

These local events allowed us to build relationships with product managers and educate the product management community about our vision. Starting a software company isn't as easy as: build product, create a marketing website, and collect money. B2B products, in particular those in a new category, require explanation and education - we're asking companies to change how they do things. We knew we'd only be as successful as product managers themselves. So alongside our investments in product, we invested in education. And we learned that it's far easier to educate a market if you've integrated into it or built a community around it.

Look at some of the top B2B software companies who've done this. Hubspot introduced and educated the world about Inbound Marketing; Gainsight built a community around the emerging customer success role; and Salesforce.com was the pioneer in cloud business software, in particular to drive revenue. Each of these companies invested heavily in nurturing and building communities to fuel their growth.

In *Great by Choice*, Jim Collins introduces the idea to "*fire bullets, then cannonballs.*"[99] One way that many great companies have leveraged this concept is to run low-cost, low-impact experiments before making a major bet. This was Pendo's approach to community building. We started by attending ProductCamps. Then we invested in our own product management community called ProductCraft. While these efforts were successful, we wanted to take a bigger bet. By joining forces with an existing community, we could:

1. bolster the size and scope of our own, and

2. add talent to our team with a history and understanding of how to build thriving communities.

This thesis is what led us to Mind the Product. Mind the Product had grown from meetups to a sizable product management community with deep international roots. The cannonball of Pendo joining forces with Mind the Product established Pendo as a key steward of a leading product management community and helped expand our community footprint internationally. We're proud and excited to carry on the tradition of Mind the Product and ensure it stays true to its roots — as its roots are grounded in the same values as Pendo.

ACKNOWLEDGMENT

The journey behind this book touched thousands of people, and there were a huge number who came together to make this book possible. We'd like to offer our thanks to all of you, and also apologies to anyone who may have been missed! It's been quite the adventure, thank you all!

First to the whole Mind the Product team and our global family of collaborators. We had an epic decade together, growing from a thing that we worked on evenings and weekends, then initially just a couple of staff to finally a full-time team of over a dozen. Running the ProductTank meetups and MTPCon conference events in so many locations really did give us the opportunity to travel the world together, and when the events world came crashing down with Covid in March 2020 we continued to work together. More than that, though, we supported one another and found ways to overcome that challenging time. Different members of the team came to the fore as different challenges arose, and I want to say in over thirty years of work, I've never had more respect for the way a group has looked out for their colleagues and gone hard together to deliver excellence for customers. It was a genuine honour to work with you all and the adventure of a lifetime.

To my co-author, Kiri Nowak-Smith! My Mind the Product journey was over a decade, and I knew early on that it would be a book worth writing. Without her partnership and writing skills, it never would have happened, so thanks to Kiri for helping bring my vision to life. If you'd like to tell your story, she's the person to go to. The book has changed over the course of our work together from a collection of Mind the Product stories to something more broad-reaching, something that can support the work of community leaders everywhere. I'm so proud of what we've been able to achieve together.

In the words of Airbnb's Co-founder and CEO,

> *"We're probably living in the loneliest time in human history, we need to rebuild physical community."*
>
> —Brian Chesky[2]

I agree wholeheartedly with him, and hopefully, this book inspires and empowers a few more to take up that challenge and seek its rewards.

Kiri also worked with a member of her writing team on this (Harriet), who worked on a few chapters with her and would like to thank her for her input. The book cover was designed by Hannah Cook.

I'd like to thank all the other people who contributed to this project! Kiri and I wanted to make sure this offered readers more than just the Mind the Product story, and to that end, spent time conducting interviews to add those voices.

A special thanks to these fine community builders!

- Namrata Sarmah of Women in Product
- Danny Hope of UX Brighton
- Vicky Twomey-Lee of Py Ladies Dublin
- Guido Lonetti of ProductTank & Mind the Product
- Fiona MacNeill of Ladies that UX Brighton

To our proofreaders - C. Todd Lombardo, Pradip Khakar. Thank you for taking this manuscript in earlier forms and playing your part in shaping this.

I'd like to thank Julius Solaris: author of the wonderful foreword and a wonderful thinker on the future of the events industry. A man who's had an outsize influence on my world.

To my partner, family, children and co-founders. Those who know my backstory will already know, this book mostly came together during the first half of 2024, which is also the period during which I was diagnosed with a brain tumour and did battle. It was a tough period for all of us, and I wouldn't have come through this time and also been able to continue the work on this book without their support.

For my mother, Pauline Mayes. She knew I was writing this, but sadly passed away a month before completion. She gave me the energy and willpower to get through more than most, forever grateful Mum. Rest well.

ABOUT THE AUTHOR

JAMES MAYES

James is a seasoned business leader with over 15 years of experience building high-performance teams across startups, banking, and tech giants. As a co-founder of Mind the Product, he helped grow it into the leading events and media brand in Product Management, achieving a truly global reach. His first book shares the blueprint for this journey, along with many actionable tips for others looking to replicate his success. It also sets the stage for his next venture: an event and community platform called Rodeo.

ABOUT THE AUTHOR

Kiri Nowak-Smith

Kiri is a senior freelance writer and master storyteller with a degree in Sociology. She's been working in content marketing, SEO, and digital marketing for over 15 years. She's CEO of The Content Wolves Ltd., a copywriting and online content company. Kiri has written copy for brands including The AA, Avis, Moonpig, Hotels.com, UNICEF and Debenhams. In the last five years, she's worked with several entrepreneurs to make their dreams of releasing a business book become a reality. Her first book as a co-author is an essential guide for anyone wishing to grow a meetup into a fully-fledged community.

REFERENCES

Preface

1
https://www.linkedin.com/in/jmayes/

◆ ◆ ◆

Acknowledgment

2
Chesky, B. (2023, June 23). "We're probably living in the loneliest time in human history, we need to rebuild physical community." In S. Mollman, Airbnb CEO says this is 'loneliest time in human history' and we need to 'rebuild physical community'. Fortune. https://fortune.com/2023/06/23/airbnb-ceo-brian-chesky-commercial-real-estate-loneliest-time-in-human-history/

◆ ◆ ◆

The Origin Story: From a small pub meetup to worldwide events…

3
Mind the Product. 2010. https://www.mindtheproduct.com/

4
McElroy, N. H. (1931). Brand man memo. Procter &

Gamble.
https://commons.wikimedia.org/wiki/File:Neil_Mcelroy%27s_1931_Brand_Man_Memo.pdf

5
Eriksson, M. (2010). Founding of ProductTank. https://www.mindtheproduct.com/refreshing-the-mind-the-product-brand-for-the-next-decade/

6
Meetup. (n.d.). ProductTank event. Meetup. https://www.meetup.com/producttank/events/13338444/

7
Bastow, J. (n.d.). Janna Bastow | LinkedIn. LinkedIn. https://uk.linkedin.com/in/jannabastow

8
Cast, S. (n.d.). Simon Cast | LinkedIn. LinkedIn. https://www.linkedin.com/in/simoncast

9
BarCamp. (n.d.). In Wikipedia. https://en.wikipedia.org/wiki/BarCamp

10
Hobbs, M. (n.d.). Matt Hobbs | LinkedIn. LinkedIn. https://uk.linkedin.com/in/hobbsmatt

11
Hadzibabic, S. (n.d.). Selena Hadzibabic | LinkedIn. LinkedIn. https://www.linkedin.com/in/selena/

12
Abraham, M. (n.d.). Marc Abraham | LinkedIn. LinkedIn. https://www.linkedin.com/in/abrahammarc/

13
Gigaom. (2015). Gigaom ceases operations. https://www.nytimes.com/2015/03/19/technology/personaltech/digital-media-darlings-unfazed-by-the-fall-of-the-news-site-gigaom.html

14
Mind the Product. (2015). Mind the Product San Francisco 2015 conference. https://www.mindtheproduct.com/conferences/san-francisco-2015/

15
ProductTank Hamburg. (2017). ProductTank Hamburg - Meetup. https://www.meetup.com/producttank-hamburg/

16
Mind the Product. (2017-2022). MTP Engage Hamburg https://www.mindtheproduct.com/mtpengage/hamburg/

17
Lombardo, C. T. (n.d.). C. Todd Lombardo | LinkedIn. LinkedIn. https://www.linkedin.com/in/toddlombardo

◆ ◆ ◆

James Mayes: My Story

18
Bryant, S. (2024, June 24). How many startups fail and why. Investopedia. https://www.investopedia.com/articles/personal-finance/040915/how-many-startups-fail-and-why.asp

19
Eisenmann, T. (2021). Why start-ups fail. Harvard Business Review. https://hbr.org/2021/05/why-start-ups-fail

20
Butcher, M. (2022, February 1). Pendo acquires Mind the Product to boost global product manager community. TechCrunch. https://techcrunch.com/2022/02/01/pendo-acquires-the-mind-the-product-to-boost-global-product-manager-community/

21
https://howdy.rodeo/organizer/

◆ ◆ ◆

Build Your Own Community: A Nine Step ACTION PLAN BLUEPRINT

22
https://howdy.rodeo/organizer/

◆ ◆ ◆

Why Meetups Matter?

23
Axtell, P. (2015). Meetings Matter: 8 Powerful Strategies for Remarkable Conversations. Jackson Creek Press. https://www.jacksoncreekpress.com/books/meetings-matter-8-powerful-strategies-for-remarkable-conversations/

24
Standout CV. (2023). Remote working statistics UK 2024 | Updated regularly. https://standout-cv.com/remote-working-statistics-uk

25
Sperling, R., Chua, E., Cocchiarella, A., Rand-Giovannetti, E., Poldrack, R., Schacter, D. L., & Albert, M. (2003). Putting names to faces: Successful encoding of associative memories activates the anterior hippocampal formation. NeuroImage, 20(2), 1400-1410. https://doi.org/10.1016/S1053-8119(03)00391-4

26
HelpGuide. (2024). Nonverbal communication: The importance of body language. https://www.helpguide.org/articles/relationships-communication/nonverbal-communication.htm

27
Navarro, J. (2008). What Every BODY is Saying: An Ex-FBI Agent's Guide to Speed-Reading People. Harper Collins.

https://www.harpercollins.com/products/what-every-body-is-saying-joe-navarromarvin-karlins?variant=32205407092770

28
Groundwork. (n.d.). Benefits of meeting in person. https://groundwork.space/benefits-of-meeting-in-person/

29
Michalski, C. A., Diemert, L. M., Helliwell, J. F., Goel, V., & Rosella, L. C. (2020). Relationship between sense of community belonging and self-rated health across life stages. SSM - Population Health, 12, 100676. https://doi.org/10.1016/j.ssmph.2020.100676

30
Harvard T.H. Chan School of Public Health. (2019). An active social life may help you live longer. https://www.hsph.harvard.edu/news/hsph-in-the-news/active-social-life-longevity/

◆ ◆ ◆

How to Host Your First Event

31
Van der Wagen, L. (2010). Event management (4th ed.). Pearson Higher Education AU. https://books.google.co.uk/books?id=zQfiBAAAQBAJ&lpg=PP1&pg=PP1

32
Weinstein, A. (2005). Handbook of niche marketing: Principles and practice (1st ed.). Routledge. https://www.routledge.com/Handbook-of-Niche-Marketing-Principles-and-Practice/Weinstein/p/book/9780789023308

33
Parker, N. (n.d.). Identify your niche and dominate it. And when I say dominate, I just mean work harder than anyone else could possibly work at it. In 130 Of The Best Marketing

Quotes That Will Get You Inspired. CoSchedule. https://coschedule.com/blog/marketing-quotes

34
OpinionX. (n.d.). OpinionX — Free stack ranking surveys. https://www.opinionx.co/

35
Superevent. (2018, December 26). 11 steps to host an effective networking event. https://superevent.com/blog/11-steps-host-effective-networking-event

36
Schreiter, T. (2013). Ice breakers! How to get any prospect to beg you for a presentation. Fortune Network Publishing Incorporated. https://www.google.co.uk/books/edition/Ice_Breakers/A9TBDwAAQBAJ?hl=en&gbpv=0

37
Manchester Young Professionals. (2022, July 12). How to host a successful networking event in 7 simple steps. https://www.mcryoungprofessionals.com/how-to-host-a-successful-networking-event/

38
https://www.mindtheproduct.com/?s=producttank%20video

39
Allen, J. (2002). The business of event planning: Behind-the-scenes secrets of successful special events. Wiley. https://www.wiley.com/en-us/The+Business+of+Event+Planning%3A+Behind+the+Scenes+Secrets+of+Successful+Special+Events-p-9780470831885

40
Kreijns, K., Kirschner, P., & Jochems, W. (2003). Identifying the pitfalls for social interaction in computer-supported collaborative learning environments: A review of

the research. Computers in Human Behavior, 19, 335-353. https://doi.org/10.1016/S0747-5632(02)00057-2

41
Jackson, N. (2013). Promoting and marketing events: Theory and practice. Taylor & Francis. https://doi.org/10.4324/9780203583166

◆ ◆ ◆

The ANATOMY of a Successful Conference

42
Sobitan, A., & Vlachos, P. (2020). Immersive event experience and attendee motivation: A quantitative analysis using sensory, localisation, and participatory factors. Journal of Policy Research in Tourism, Leisure and Events. https://doi.org/10.1080/19407963.2020.1721638

43
Kim, Y. S., Lee, Y. Y., & Love, C. (2009). A Case Study Examining the Influence of Conference Food Function on Attendee Satisfaction and Return Intention at a Corporate Conference. Journal of Convention & Event Tourism, 10(3), 211–230. https://doi.org/10.1080/15470140903178567

44
Kim, Y. S., Lee, Y. Y., & Love, C. (2009). A Case Study Examining the Influence of Conference Food Function on Attendee Satisfaction and Return Intention at a Corporate Conference. Journal of Convention & Event Tourism, 10(3), 211–230. https://doi.org/10.1080/15470140903178567

45
Global Conference Alliance Inc. (n.d.). Global Conference Alliance Inc. https://globalconference.ca

46
Foster, M. I., & Keane, M. T. (2018). The role of surprise in learning: Different surprising outcomes affect memorability differentially. Topics in Cognitive Science, 11(1), 1–15. https://doi.org/10.1111/tops.12392

47
Heath, C., & Heath, D. (2017). The power of moments: Why certain experiences have extraordinary impact. Simon & Schuster. https://www.amazon.co.uk/Power-Moments-Certain-Experiences-Extraordinary/dp/0593079264

48
ICC Belfast. (n.d.). 10 considerations for choosing an event venue. https://iccbelfast.com/blogs/10-considerations-for-choosing-an-event-venue

49
An, J., Kim, H., & Hur, D. (2021). Keeping the competitive edge of a convention and exhibition center in MICE environment: Identification of event attributes for long-run success. Sustainability, 13(9), 5030. https://doi.org/10.3390/su13095030

◆ ◆ ◆

Growth: How to Take Your Community from 20 People to 300,000

50
Keller, H. (1980). Helen and Teacher: The Story of Helen Keller and Anne Sullivan Macy (J. P. Lash, Ed.). Delacorte Press.

51
Forsyth, D. R. (2019). The Psychology of Groups. In R. Biswas-Diener & E. Diener (Eds.), Noba textbook series: Psychology. Champaign, IL: DEF publishers. https://nobaproject.com/modules/the-psychology-of-groups

52
Forsyth, D. R. (2019). The Psychology of Groups. In R. Biswas-Diener & E. Diener (Eds.), Noba textbook series: Psychology. Champaign, IL: DEF publishers. https://nobaproject.com/modules/the-psychology-of-groups

53
Parents. (n.d.). What toddler social development looks like. https://www.parents.com/toddlers-preschoolers/development/social/social-development-milestones-ages-1-to-4/

54
Parents. (n.d.). What toddler social development looks like. https://www.parents.com/toddlers-preschoolers/development/social/social-development-milestones-ages-1-to-4/

55
Slack, T. (n.d.). Passion and enthusiasm: Why they're the key to strategic planning. Appreciating People. https://appreciatingpeople.co.uk/passion-and-enthusiasm-why-theyre-the-key-to-strategic-planning/

56
Liu, Q., Shao, Z., & Fan, W. (2018). The impact of users' sense of belonging on social media habit formation: Empirical evidence from social networking and microblogging websites in China. Computers in Human Behavior, 85, 1-10. https://doi.org/10.1016/j.chb.2018.03.022

57
Avinoam, B., May, A., & Yu, D. (2016). The motivations, enablers and barriers for voluntary participation in an online crowdsourcing platform. Computers in Human Behavior, 68, 503-510. https://doi.org/10.1016/j.chb.2016.11.045

58
Ratanakosol, K., Pathumcharoenwattana, W., & Kimpee, P. (2016). Learning process for creating community identity. SHS Web of Conferences, 26, 01067. https://doi.org/10.1051/shsconf/20162601067

59
Blanchard, A. L., & Markus, M. L. (2004). The experienced

"sense" of a virtual community: Characteristics and processes. ACM SIGMIS Database, 35(1), 64-79. https://doi.org/10.1145/968464.96847

60
TheoryHub. (n.d.). Social comparison theory. https://open.ncl.ac.uk/academic-theories/34/social-comparison-theory/

61
Mills, M., Oghazi, P., Hultman, M., & Theotokis, A. (2022). The impact of brand communities on public and private brand loyalty: A field study in professional sports. Journal of Business Research, 142, 266-275. https://doi.org/10.1016/j.jbusres.2022.06.045

62
Hayes, A. (2024, July 2). Word-of-mouth marketing: Meaning and uses in business. Investopedia. https://www.investopedia.com/terms/w/word-of-mouth-marketing.asp

63
Bussgang, J., & Bacon, J. (2020, January 21). When community becomes your competitive advantage. Harvard Business Review. https://hbr.org/2020/01/when-community-becomes-your-competitive-advantage

64
Forsyth, D. R. (2019). The Psychology of Groups. In R. Biswas-Diener & E. Diener (Eds.), Noba textbook series: Psychology. Champaign, IL: DEF publishers. https://nobaproject.com/modules/the-psychology-of-groups

65
Matthews-El, T. (2024, April 17). 14 customer retention strategies that work in 2024. Forbes Advisor. https://www.forbes.com/advisor/business/customer-retention-strategies/

66

Yilmaz, R. (2016). Knowledge sharing behaviors in e-learning community: Exploring the role of academic self-efficacy and sense of community. Computers in Human Behavior, 65, 292-298. https://doi.org/10.1016/j.chb.2016.08.044

67
Lykourentzou, I., Vergados, D. J., Kapetanios, E., & Loumos, V. (2011). Collective intelligence systems: Classification and modeling. Journal of Emerging Technologies in Web Intelligence, 3(3), 217-226. https://doi.org/10.4304/jetwi.3.3.217-226

68
Best Practice Biz. (2023, March 02). Why customer trust is important for business: Citation Certification. LinkedIn. https://www.linkedin.com/pulse/why-customer-trust-important-business-best-practice-biz/

69
Blanchard, A. L., & Markus, M. L. (2004). The experienced "sense" of a virtual community: Characteristics and processes. ACM SIGMIS Database, 35(1), 64-79. https://doi.org/10.1145/968464.96847

◆ ◆ ◆

Creating Memorable Moments

70
Stenson, A. F., Leventon, J. S., & Bauer, P. J. (2019). Emotion effects on memory from childhood through adulthood: Consistent enhancement and adult gender differences. Journal of Experimental Child Psychology, 178, 121–136. https://doi.org/10.1016/j.jecp.2018.09.016

71
University of Michigan. (2007, November 1). Ten minutes of talking improves memory and test performance. ScienceDaily.

72
Buchanan, T. W. (2007). Retrieval of emotional memories. Psychological Bulletin, 133(5), 761–779. https://doi.org/10.1037/0033-2909.133.5.761

73
Fesenmaier, D. R., & Xiang, Z. (Eds.). (2016). Analytics in smart tourism design: Concepts and methods. Springer International Publishing. https://doi.org/10.1007/978-3-319-44263-1

74
Gaudini, G. C. (2019). The art of event planning: Pro tips from an industry insider. Gianna Gaudini, LLC. https://www.google.co.uk/books/edition/The_Art_of_Event_Planning/XKBJzQEACAAJ?hl=en

75
Heath, C., & Heath, D. (2017). The power of moments: Why certain experiences have extraordinary impact. Simon & Schuster. https://www.amazon.co.uk/Power-Moments-Certain-Experiences-Extraordinary/dp/0593079264

76
Destination + Group of Companies. (2023, October 28). The magic of surprise and delight: Crafting unexpected moments in events. LinkedIn. https://www.linkedin.com/pulse/magic-surprise-delight-crafting-unexpected-moments-kv3ff/

77
Meetup. (n.d.). Meetup | Find local groups, events, and activities near you. https://www.meetup.com/

◆ ◆ ◆

How to Maintain Engagement

78
Alroy, A., Ben-Shushan, E., & Katz, B. (2022). Event success: Maximizing the business impact of in-person, virtual, and hybrid experiences. Wiley.

https://www.wiley.com/en-us/Event+Success%3A+Maximizing+the+Business+Impact+of+In-person%2C+Virtual%2C+and+Hybrid+Experiences-p-9781119817161

79
Al-Rabayah, W., Khasawneh, R., Abu-shamaa, R., & Alsmadi, I. (2016). Strategic uses of social media for improved customer retention. IGI Global. https://books.google.com.ph/books/about/Strategic_Uses_of_Social_Media_for_Impro.html?id=TLWADQAAQBAJ&redir_esc=y

80
Global Nexus. (2023, August 4). The role of social media in event promotion: Expanding horizons and engaging audiences. LinkedIn. https://www.linkedin.com/pulse/role-social-media-event-promotion-expanding-horizons-engaging/

81
Entrepreneur Media, & Kimball, C. (2015). Start your own event planning business: Your step-by-step guide to success. Entrepreneur Press. https://books.google.com.ph/books/about/Start_Your_Own_Event_Planning_Business.html?id=5gL3BwAAQBAJ&redir_esc=y

82
Jackson, N. (2008). MPs and their e-Newsletters: Winning Votes by Promoting Constituency Service. The Journal of Legislative Studies, 14(4), 488–499. https://doi.org/10.1080/13572330802442923

83
Jackson, N. (2013). Promoting and marketing events: Theory and practice. Routledge. https://doi.org/10.4324/9780203583166

◆ ◆ ◆

Community Case Studies

84
www.wip-uk.com

85
https://www.linkedin.com/company/women-in-product-uk

86
https://www.facebook.com/groups/190072394960873/

◆ ◆ ◆

How to Develop Commercial Sustainability

87
Bartlett, S. (2023). The diary of a CEO: The 33 laws of business and life. Portfolio. https://www.amazon.com/Diary-CEO-Laws-Business-Life/dp/0593715837

88
Intribe. (2022, July 13). Brand fails: The worst partnerships ever. Intribe Blog. https://www.intribe.co/blog/brand-fails-the-worst-partnerships-ever

89
Mind the Product. (n.d.). The Mind the Product manifesto. https://www.mindtheproduct.com/about/the-mind-the-product-manifesto/

◆ ◆ ◆

The End Game: How To Sell Your Community Business

90
Davidson, B. I., Jones, S. L., Joinson, A. N., & Hinds, J. (2019). The evolution of online ideological communities. PLOS ONE, 14(5), e0216932.

https://doi.org/10.1371/journal.pone.0216932

91
Butcher, M. (2022, February 1). Pendo acquires Mind the Product to boost global product manager community. TechCrunch. https://techcrunch.com/2022/02/01/pendo-acquires-the-mind-the-product-to-boost-global-product-manager-community/

92
Gainsight. (2022, January 10). Gainsight acquires community software leader inSided. https://www.gainsight.com/press/gainsight-acquires-insided/

93
Collingwood Group. (n.d.). Collingwood: Homepage. https://collingwood.group/

94
Ryzhkov, A. (2024, August 20). How to sell online community business in 9 steps: Checklist. Finmodels Lab. https://finmodelslab.com/blogs/sell-business/online-community

◆ ◆ ◆

In Conclusion...

95
Andreessen, M. (2011, August 20). Why software is eating the world. The Wall Street Journal. https://www.wsj.com/articles/SB10001424053111903480904576512250915629460

96
Mind the Product. (n.d.). Product ethics. https://www.mindtheproduct.com/category/product-ethics/

◆ ◆ ◆

Afterword

97
Olson, T. (n.d.). Todd Olson - CEO / Founder at Pendo. LinkedIn. https://www.linkedin.com/in/toddaolson/

98
Pendo. 2013. https://www.pendo.io/

99
Collins, J., & Hansen, M. T. (2011). Great by choice: Uncertainty, chaos, and luck—Why some thrive despite them all. HarperCollins.

Table of Contents

Printed in Great Britain
by Amazon

61372195R00117